T0319104

Cambridge Elements ≡

Elements in Translation and Interpreting
edited by
Kirsten Malmkjær
University of Leicester

INTERPRETING AS TRANSLANGUAGING

Theory, Research, and Practice

Lili Han
Macao Polytechnic University

Zhisheng (Edward) Wen
Hong Kong Shue Yan University

Alan James Runcieman
University of Vic - Central University of Catalonia

CAMBRIDGE
UNIVERSITY PRESS

CAMBRIDGE
UNIVERSITY PRESS

Shaftesbury Road, Cambridge CB2 8EA, United Kingdom

One Liberty Plaza, 20th Floor, New York, NY 10006, USA

477 Williamstown Road, Port Melbourne, VIC 3207, Australia

314–321, 3rd Floor, Plot 3, Splendor Forum, Jasola District Centre,
New Delhi – 110025, India

103 Penang Road, #05–06/07, Visioncrest Commercial, Singapore 238467

Cambridge University Press is part of Cambridge University Press & Assessment,
a department of the University of Cambridge.

We share the University's mission to contribute to society through the pursuit of
education, learning and research at the highest international levels of excellence.

www.cambridge.org
Information on this title: www.cambridge.org/9781009462631

DOI: 10.1017/9781009375870

© Lili Han, Zhisheng (Edward) Wen, and Alan James Runcieman 2023

This publication is in copyright. Subject to statutory exception and to the provisions
of relevant collective licensing agreements, no reproduction of any part may take
place without the written permission of Cambridge University Press & Assessment.

First published 2023

A catalogue record for this publication is available from the British Library

ISBN 978-1-009-46263-1 Hardback
ISBN 978-1-009-37589-4 Paperback
ISSN 2633-6480 (online)
ISSN 2633-6472 (print)

Cambridge University Press & Assessment has no responsibility for the persistence
or accuracy of URLs for external or third-party internet websites referred to in this
publication and does not guarantee that any content on such websites is, or will
remain, accurate or appropriate.

Interpreting as Translanguaging

Theory, Research, and Practice

Elements in Translation and Interpreting

DOI: 10.1017/9781009375870
First published online: October 2023

Lili Han
Macao Polytechnic University

Zhisheng (Edward) Wen
Hong Kong Shue Yan University

Alan James Runcieman
University of Vic - Central University of Catalonia

Author for correspondence: Lili Han, hanlili@mpu.edu.mo

Abstract: Drawing on the emerging literature in translanguaging theory and research, the Element provides a comprehensive analysis of the embedded model of translanguaging-in-interpreting and interpreting-in-translanguaging from theoretical and practical perspectives, buttressed by evidence from an exploratory empirical investigation. To achieve this goal, the authors first trace the emergence and historical development of the key concepts and basic tenets of translanguaging and interpreting separately and then combined. This is followed by reviews of relevant literature, synthesizing how translanguaging theories and research methods can be applied in specific domains of interpreting studies, such as community and public service interpreting. An integrated account of translanguaging and interpreting is proposed and elaborated. The theoretical and methodological implications of this integrative perspective are teased out, with a view to illuminating interpreting theory, pedagogy, and instruction.

Keywords: interpreting, translanguaging, moment analysis, multilingualism, multimodality

© Lili Han, Zhisheng (Edward) Wen, and Alan James Runcieman 2023

ISBNs: 9781009462631 (HB), 9781009375894 (PB), 9781009375870 (OC)
ISSNs: 2633-6480 (online), 2633-6472 (print)

Contents

1 Introduction   1

2 What Is Interpreting?   9

3 Interpreting as Translanguaging: Rationale and Theoretical Foundation   15

4 Translanguaging (Spaces) in Simultaneous and Consecutive Interpreting: Moment Analysis   23

5 Translanguaging in Community/Public-Service Interpreting   46

6 Conclusion and Future Directions   54

References   55

1 Introduction

The title of this Element is *Interpreting as Translanguaging: Theory, Research, and Practice.* Let us unpack this by giving a general overview of the central issues the Element addresses and how they are approached. For many, the act of interpreting involves an oral/written transfer from *one* language/culture to another, with the aim of obtaining the closest possible equivalence between the two. However, in our increasingly globalized and superdiverse world (which we will explore in Section 1.1), this has become more and more problematic. People who have migrated to other countries have always brought with them bi-/multilingual and cultural resources that they have drawn upon when and where they are necessary for situated interlinguistic/intercultural contexts. Barriers to communication lead to individuals sourcing all their linguistic/ cultural and multimodal resources to bridge the gap when communicating with their interlocutors in order "to get things done" (Pennycook and Otsuji, 2015). Urban centers globally have become a melting pot of semiotic resources that increasingly disregard monolingual/monocultural nation-state ideologies, that is, the separation of the language/culture of the host state and the language/ culture of the immigrant community.

In this Element, we focus on the concept of "translanguaging," an increasingly observed, recorded, and analyzed means of communication in superdiverse societies, which describes how a person's linguistic and cultural experience is drawn upon, often leading to their production of a melded, hybridized, creative, and critical sourcing of all their semiotic repertoire, challenging the ideological monolingual/monocultural bias of individual nation-states.

We approach this in relation to the interpreting profession and the impact translanguaging is having on its monolingual framing of interlinguistic interactions; that is, interpreting between one nation's language and another's. This, we argue, is in dissolution, as the citizens of nation-states are increasingly multilingual/multi-cultural, and consequently, a one-for-one linguistic/cultural interchange is increas-ingly being challenged. The globalized, internationally transiting citizens of the twenty-first century are breaking down the conservative one nation, one language, one culture status quo of the past, which interpreters are still schooled in.

In this Element, we adopt two distinct albeit complementary approaches to analyzing interpreting from the translanguaging perspective. First, we take a social-cognitive approach, through which we describe the social-cognitive factors influencing the interpreting process from the translanguaging perspec-tive, including the broader social-cultural and ideological contexts (the macro level), the external environment (the meso level), and the psychological and neurobiological factors (i.e., cognitive faculties and processes analyzed from the micro level). This approach will run through Sections 2 to 4. Then, in Section 5, we switch to a different approach, that of the ethnographic perspective, which draws on the personal accounts of interpreters, and how translanguaging impacts and shapes their perceptions of practicing their profession in an increasingly multilingual/translanguaging world.

This Element posits and extends translanguaging as a broad theoretical and methodological lens to interpreting studies, by providing a thorough and insightful empirical investigation of different modes of interpreting. Translanguaging, as a theory of cognition and human communication, inspires innovative and interdisciplinary studies of interpreting and underpins the complexity of interpreting activities. The interactive dynamics of translanguaging and interpreting are seen as embedded in each other, contributing to enrich the in-depth knowledge of both.

In the following sections, we first describe the rise of superdiversity and the consequent translanguaging practices emerging in urban centers globally and what this means for interpreting. We then consider the rationale and theoretical foundations of interpreting as a translanguaging event before moving on to the different translanguaging spaces in simultaneous and consecutive interpreting. After this, we turn to look at the impact translanguaging is having on one specific form of interpreting, community/public-service interpreting. We conclude by considering future perspectives on how interpreting will be impacted in the coming years.

1.1 Superdiversity and Translanguaging

The migration of peoples has been documented throughout all recorded human history, with the consequent emergence of multilingual and multicultural communities living side by side in multiple geopolitical regions and/or nations globally (Baigorri-Jalón, 2015). However, one could argue that what is occurring more recently, due to globalization, increased international migration patterns (see United Nations, 2017: 1), and the rise of virtual communities through the Internet (Androutsopoulos and Juffermans, 2014), is that social, cultural, and linguistic diversity in societies has surpassed anything ever seen before (see McAuliffe and Triandafyllidou, 2022: 346), a complexity that has come to be known as "superdiversity" (Vertovec, 2007). This process has deep roots going back to pre-digital times, as Appadurai described and argued as early as 1996:

> The story of mass migrations (voluntary and forced) is hardly a new feature of human history. But when it is juxtaposed with the rapid flow of mass-mediated images, scripts and sensations, we have a new order of instability in the production of modern subjectivities. As Turkish guest workers in

Germany watch Turkish films in their German flats, as Koreans in Philadelphia watch the 1988 Olympics in Seoul through satellite feeds from Korea, and as Pakistani cabdrivers in Chicago listen to cassettes of sermons recorded in mosques in Pakistan or Iran, we see moving images meet deterritorialized viewers. These create diasporic public spheres, phenomena that confound theories that depend on the continued salience of the nation-state as the key arbiter of important social changes. (Appadurai, 1996: 4)

In today's world, what had already begun in the 1980s (the world of "cassettes," "VHS," and "satellite dishes") has of course been largely superseded by digital and internet technologies (e.g., Facebook, Instagram, TikTok, and most recently, ChatGPT, etc.), increasing the speed of multilingual/multicultural interactivity globally and, consequently, a far more diverse and complex set of largely unpredictable "superdiverse," postmodern subjectivities (see Androutsopoulos and Juffermans, 2014).

Superdiversity has resulted in the increasing prevalence and visibility of what has come to be known as "translanguaging" (García and Li, 2014). This is a form of intercommunication where the individual's critical and creative drive to communicate draws on multiple "languages" in melded and hybridized ways (Li, 2011a). In contrast to "codeswitching" (i.e., a crossing of "borders" between individual and discrete languages), translanguaging takes the epistemological position that all "languages" are in fact fluid and borderless (García, 2009; García and Li, 2014).

Translanguaging describes how *all* of a person's "language" (every (para) linguistic and multimodal resource) can be drawn upon as potential affordances for communication in situated contexts. Moreover, as a practice in daily life it has seen exponential growth globally (see Creese, Blackledge, and Hu, 2018; Pennycook and Otsuji, 2015).

Translanguaging is first and foremost a universally observed and recorded multi-/translingual practice, emerging principally in multiple urban contexts, in the marketplaces, shops, and various civic institutions (i.e., libraries, museums, art centers, etc.) of bustling city centers globally, from the Northern to the Southern Hemispheres (Blommaert and Rampton 2011; Creese and Blackledge 2015; Creese, Blackledge, and Hu 2018; Pennycook and Otsuji, 2015), as well as in educational institutions (García, 2009; García and Li, 2014; Kramsch and Zhang, 2018; Li, 2011a) with increasingly mixed migrant ethnicities, both generationally well-established and/or more recent arrivals.

Essentially and primarily a sociolinguistic living practice, translanguaging has also emerged as a paradigm in academia, which draws on these observed practices to develop new theories and perspectives on the ontological and epistemological dimensions of language and to challenge existing ideologies.

Among its range of interests is how this fluid, hybrid, and creative form of multilingualism is breaking down the conceptual framing of languages as being individual and bounded entities, by seeing all "language" as a borderless set of multiple, semiotic resources that an individual can access in situated communication (Li, 2011a). Such an approach is also seen in pedagogy as promoting higher cognitive development by allowing individuals to draw on all their linguistic resources when engaging in critical thinking (García and Li, 2014).

Translanguaging has also turned its gaze to "the complex ways in which fluid and fixed, as well as global and local, practices reconstitute language and identities" (Otsuji and Pennycook, 2010: 247),[1] how it can

> [d]escribe the ways in which people of different and mixed backgrounds use, play with and negotiate identities through language; it does not assume connections between language, culture, ethnicity, nationality, or geography, but rather seeks to explore how such relations are produced, resisted, defied, or rearranged; its focus is not on language systems but on languages as emergent from contexts of interaction. (246)

Moreover, translanguaging has also taken a postcolonial critical path, questioning and contesting postcolonial linguistic hierarchies based on ingrained sociopolitical discourses that have historically diminished the importance of minority languages (García, 2009). Indeed, much research has emerged that challenges ideologies of class, race, and gender superiority in multilingual societies (i.e., García, Flores, and Spotti, 2017).

Although translanguaging has acquired these specific academic trajectories, it is principally concerned with examining the interchangeable "spontaneous, impromptu, and momentary actions and performances" (Li, 2011a: 1224) of multilinguals in situated speech. In this sense, it can be seen as a form of "multilingualism from below" (Pennycook and Otsuji, 2015), as it seeks to describe how "language is used by people to interact, as an extension of their own humanity, not always according to the rules and definitions of language by political and social institutions. Translanguaging privileges unbounded and agentive dynamic and fluid use of bilinguals' entire linguistic repertoire" (García and Kleifgen, 2019: 557). Translanguaging is both a practice and a process, a practice of integrating different languages and varieties "but more importantly a process *of knowledge construction* that goes beyond language(s)" (Li, 2018: 15; original emphasis).

---

[1] Although Pennycook and Otsuji frame this as part of what they refer to as "metrolingualism," Li and Zhu (2013) have taken a similar position with regard to "translanguaging."

1.2 Historical Emergence of Translanguaging as a Theoretical Concept in Academia

The original concept and term "translanguaging" emerged with the Welsh academic Cen Williams' doctoral thesis (Williams, 1994). This thesis was based on how already observable bilingual practices in secondary education could be instrumentalized as pedagogical tools to aid students in their cognitive development.

Initially an interchange between literacy and oral production, *trawsieithu* (Williams' original Welsh term, later translated into English by Baker (2003) as "translanguaging") represented classroom activities that involved students reading in one language, Welsh or English (as input), and their discussions in another, Welsh or English (as output), which the research argued showed a marked improvement in students' cognitive uptake.

Although Baker did not specify the origin of the word "translanguaging" (he had originally translated it as "translingualling"), Li (2018) reflects that it would seem to be aligned with the concept of "languaging." "Languaging" first emerged in the fields of biology and neuroscience (Maturana and Varela, 1980) and was later adopted by the linguist Anton Becker (1991) to frame language as a continually evolving process and a transformational human activity (and therefore better represented by a gerund), in contrast to a static, monolithic entity (represented instead by a concrete noun).

The prefix "trans" has been variously framed by different authors. Hawkins and Mori (2018) see it as part of interdisciplinary research into the effects of globalization and a need to *trans*cend named and bounded categories (i.e., transnational, transgender, transculturation). García and Li (2014), as well as García and Kleifgen (2019), see "trans" as representative of a *transversal* movement, as well as of the concepts of *transcendence* and *transformation*, in the context of second language acquisition and bilingual education, concerned specifically with overcoming the limitations of seeing languages as fixed and bounded artifacts and the need to change educational approaches, particularly with regard to bi-/multilingualism in the classroom.

From Williams' (1994) initial study of how combined bilingual oral and literacy approaches to learning could improve cognitive uptake, much of translanguaging's early historical development in the academy emerged from the field of (bi)literacy studies (García and Kleifgen, 2019). In 1996, the New London Group first proposed "a pedagogy of multiliteracies consisting of situated practice, overt instruction, critical framing, and transformed practice" (García and Kleifgen, 2019: 553). This multiliteracy perspective was driven in part by the rise of the Internet in multimodal global communication, with its new visual, gestural, and audial forms of expression. In parallel, the concept of "multiliteracies" was also developed by the New Literacies paradigm (Street, 1984), which engaged in ethnographic studies to reveal other forms of socioculturally varied global literacies, as part of localized social practice(s), that did not necessarily conform to more narrow Western concepts of what counted as literacy.

Specifically, in the field of biliteracy studies, Cummins (1979) first posited the existence of a shared cognitive pool of resources in both primary and secondary language acquisition, which he dubbed "interdependence theory," highlighting the shared and transferrable cognitive skills that existed between languages. Later, Hornberger (1989) would propose that biliteracy educators should recognize the perceptible sourcing of the "mobile and multiple" communicative repertoires of their students, valuing and building on them in their pedagogy. However, despite these important shifts in perspective, languages were still being considered separate psycholinguistic entities, and bilingualism continued to be envisaged as a kind of crossing and/or bridging between the two (García and Kleifgen, 2019).

Vivian Cook's (1992) concept of "multi-competence" in the field of applied linguistics was the first real step toward seeing languages not only as sharing interrelated resources but as actually existing in the same interconnected cognitive space. Before Cook, second language acquisition was positioned as an inferior addition to an individual's primary language (i.e., LA + LB), treated primarily as an example of monolingual deficiency (cf. Grosjean, 1982). Cook, instead, argued that it was rather a holistic incorporation of another set of linguistic resources that altered and enriched the individual's perception of the world, extending and amplifying all their means of communication.

The next significant came educational linguistics with Van Lier's (2008) introduction of the "ecological perspective" on languages, which broadened the debate about cognition and language and highlighted the complex interconnectivity between humans and their physical environment. This perspective saw all languages as providing polysemiotic and interrelated resources and affordances, for more diverse goals and objectives than the reductive acquisition of individual, bounded, and discrete languages (see Kramsch and Zhang, 2018).

More recently, a "multilingual turn" (May, 2013; Meier, 2017; Meier and Conteh, 2014) has emerged in language pedagogy, with proponents arguing for a significant change in approaches to multilingualism, where language learners are firmly positioned "as diverse multilingual and social practitioners; and learning as a multilingual social practice based on theoretical pluralism, consistently guided by critical perspectives" (Meier, 2017: 131). The multilingual turn (as well as translanguaging theories) has also had a significant influence on the Common European Framework of Reference for Languages (CEFR), the internationally influential framework for language user/learner pedagogy and evaluation processes, and its recent advocation of "plurilingual spaces" in informal mediatory contexts (see Council of Europe, 2020). Here, all of a language user's/learner's linguistic resources are considered valid and relevant in facilitating a plurilingual vision of communication in the postmodern world (for a critique, see Runcieman, 2023).[2]

Now, with translanguaging's firm establishment as an academic paradigm, theoretical and methodological approaches to it are fast emerging in research into education. One such example, in language pedagogy in Spain, has been the Integrated Plurilingual Approach (IPA), a project for language teaching and learning pedagogy that aims to teach additional languages from plurilingual, communicative, and conceptual perspectives (see Esteve and González-Davies, 2017).

1.3 Overview of the Structure of the Element

Given the emerging body of empirical studies in interpreting research through the translanguaging lens, the need for a more comprehensive and updated volume providing guidelines for conceptualizing and measuring this fundamental embedded construct has become urgent. This need gives rise to this Element. Coauthored by the original proponents of the three most dominant translanguaging-in-interpreting/interpreting-in-translanguaging models (Runcieman, Han, and Wen), it will hopefully provide authoritative insights and shed new light on key issues in theory, research, and practice related to both translanguaging and interpreting.

Following this introductory section, Sections 2 and 3 explain key concepts of translanguaging and interpreting respectively. Specifically, they review major translanguaging-in-interpreting/interpreting-in-translanguaging theories and models, culminating in a unified understanding of translanguaging as a methodological apparatus to understand the multimodal, multisemiotic, and multilingual dynamics of interpreting by means of meaning-making. These two sections will particularly focus on two dominant aspects, namely the seminal translanguaging theory proposed by Li (e.g., Li 2011a, 2018), key features of which are translanguaging space and liminal moments, and the embedded

---

[2] Although the CEFR conflates "plurilingual" practices with translanguaging, there are still divergences between the two, as plurilingualism perceives multilingualism as a mixing of multiple "named languages" (i.e., LA, LB, LC) whereas translanguaging contests that naming and advocates all language as a borderless resource allowing for critical and creative, melded, and hybrid forms of communication (Runcieman, 2023).

translanguaging-in-interpreting/interpreting-in-translanguaging model initiated by Baynham and Lee (2019), developed and strengthened by Runcieman (2021), and further broadened and elaborated by Han and colleagues (2023). We will trace their pedigrees and summarize the breakthrough development, paving the way for more detailed discussions in the next section.

The reviews in Sections 2 and 3 culminate in the main developments in conceptualizing and measuring translanguaging in interpreting from macro, meso, and micro perspectives. In essence, this three-layered translanguaging-informed interpreting model (the 3M Model) conceptualizes and depicts the interpreting process as the fluid, dynamic, and complex interactions with the interpreter's individual-based multicompetence (at the micro level), blended with those multimodal affordances in the external environment (at the meso level), as well as the broader sociocultural contexts in which the interpreting practice is situated and embodied (at the macro level).

In Section 4, we argue that such a translanguaging lens for interpreting, when augmented by integrated research methods from neighboring disciplines such as the dynamic systems approach from applied linguistics, allows us to simulate, explain, and predict adequately the emergence, real-time performance, and developmental trajectories of interpreting. The 3M Model is put into practice in this section. We demonstrate how the interpreting process is considered a highly complex and dynamic activity that engages the interpreter's cognition, emotion, and action during successive "translanguaging moments" of meaning-making (i.e., interpreting-in-translanguaging). Alternatively, as interpreting entails distinct time sensitivity and consumes different amounts of cognitive resources at different stages, the interpreters' momentary engagement is analyzed through the translanguaging lens, with a view to probing their underlying nonlinearity, self-organization, and emergence dynamics from a micro-level perspective (i.e., translanguaging-in-interpreting). "Moment analysis" (cf. Li, 2011a; Lee, 2022) will emerge to prominence in the end as a viable and powerful research method for interpreting-as-translanguaging research.

Section 5 adopts a slightly different approach by probing into the pedagogical implications of translanguaging-in-interpreting/interpreting-in-translanguaging derived from current translanguaging-interpreting explorations (i.e., the 3M Model). We argue that interpreter training needs to respond to superdiversity and translanguaging, as future interpreters are part of the same social world and will undoubtedly encounter translanguaging in their future professional life. In superdiverse and translanguaging societies, source and target languages are no longer a one-to-one linguistic and cultural translation but a far more fluid, dynamic, and multiple interchange of repertoires and resources that people access in multivaried and multifunctional ways.

In this increasingly complex scenario, languages are not seen as bounded entities but rather as fluid and interchangeable in the situated moment, and this, it is argued, needs to be reflected in pedagogy. Moreover, translanguaging (between bi-/multilinguals) has been shown to promote greater cognitive development when tackling complex issues and rationalizing processes. In addition, translanguaging aids social and professional identity work, as interpreter students develop their understandings of the role their future interpreter life can and needs to play in their career.

Finally, Section 6 concludes the Element by briefly recapitulating the reviews in the previous sections. It then proposes new avenues for future research, investigating the relationship between translanguaging and interpreting, couched within the newly proposed 3M Model. For example, regarding the macro, meso, and micro levels, we call for more empirical research to explore the model's relation to other competencies each level (i.e., the aptitude) and complex dynamic systems. Then, regarding the embedded translanguaging-in-interpreting/interpreting-in-translanguaging model, suggestions are made to clarify relation to interpreting aptitude and to complex and dynamic systems.

2 What Is Interpreting?

Many well-articulated objectives of foreign-language education programs have included the mastery of five language skills: listening, speaking, reading, writing, and translating/interpreting. Among these targets, translating/interpreting is undeniably one of the most complex meaning-making activities, implicating a broad range of linguistic skills and social-cognitive processes (cf. Larson, 1984; Levý, 1967/2018). However, as a millennia-old practice that emerged as a profession only in the twentieth century, translation and interpreting came into their own as a subject of academic study and ultimately crystallized as the translation studies discipline in the 1970s with the famous seminal article by Holmes (1972), "The name and nature of translation studies." Originally presented in 1972 to the translation section of the Third International Congress of Applied Linguistics in Copenhagen, the article was later published in 1988 (Holmes, 1988: 67–80). It outlines the field of what Holmes termed "translation studies" and its two main objectives: "to describe the phenomena of translating and translation(s) as they manifest themselves in the world of our experience" and "to establish general principles by means of which these phenomena can be explained and predicted" (71). Since Holmes' paper, translation studies has evolved to an extent that it has turned interdisciplinary, interwoven with many other fields. According to Pöchhacker (2016: 10),

"Within the conceptual structure of translation, interpreting can be distinguished from other types of translational activity most succinctly by its immediacy: in principle, interpreting is performed "here and now" for the benefit of people who want to engage in communication across barriers of language and culture." In light of this conceptual outline, interpreting is approached in our Element from the perspective of translation studies.

With the burgeoning research enthusiasm for translating and interpreting studies in past decades, many theoretical discussions and empirical investigations have been conducted, offering clearer clues to the different facets of translating and interpreting aptitude. Notwithstanding these discussions and investigations, the field still needs a unified theory and is in dire need of an operational aptitude model to explain and predict translation products and interpreting processes and to encapsulate the broad range of complex interplaying factors that are at work during the different timescales (e.g., before, during, and after) implicated in the translation/interpreting activity.

After its development over several decades, the field of translating and interpreting has witnessed a growth in theoretical perspectives and models (Setton, 2012). That said, most of the previous models of translating and interpreting are constantly updating conceptualizations and interpretations of the multiple facets of the translating and interpreting process and products, as a response to the evolving perspectives and changing paradigms in translation/interpreting studies. For example, in line with the six developmental stages in cognitive translating and interpreting studies (Alves and Jakobsen, 2021), research paradigms have adjusted accordingly from the early product-oriented text-linguistic traditions focusing on the performance and products of translating and interpreting to the now more prevalent approaches tapping the cognitive processes of translating and interpreting (Alves, 2003; Li, Lei, and He, 2019). These paradigm shifts in cognitive translation studies have given rise to the development of vibrant and successive "turns" in translation/interpreting studies (Pöchhacker, 2016, 2022).

These epistemic "turns" in translating and interpreting studies, such as the "sociological turn," the "cognitive turn," and the more recent "neural network turn," as well as the "technological turn," all represent distinctive research focuses that have illuminated selective aspects of the translation/interpreting process, products, and training. Within each research paradigm, theoretical perspectives and models are formulated and take shape gradually, becoming the referential norm for some time until a newer "turn" develops. For example, theoretical models belonging to the "sociological turn" have highlighted the communicative interaction among translators/interpreters within the social-cultural environment. These include the Role Model by Alexieva (1997), which addresses the multiparameter typology of interpreting constellations, and the Participation Model by Wadensjö (1998), which is derived from Goffman's (1981) model, and conceptualizes interpreter agency from a sociological approach.

Other cognitively oriented models have taken a slightly different route by focusing on mental operations during the translation/interpreting process. They include: the early cognitive short-term and working memory models by Gerver (1976), Moser (1978), and (later) the Paris School (Seleskovitch and Lederer, 2002); the embodied, embedded, enacted, extended, and affective (4 EA) cognition approach (Muñoz Martín, 2010); Seeber's (2011) cognitive load model; and the noteworthy Effort Models of interpreting developed by Gile (1985, 1995/2009). The latter is a series of refined models that focus on depicting the interpreter's cognitive load and efforts implicated in receptive and productive stages and skills during interpreting. That said, these models were initially intended for simultaneous interpreting (SI) but were later expanded to explain sight interpreting and consecutive interpreting (CI) as well. Then, in the latest "neural network turn" and "technological turn," in which most technology-savvy computational and big data knowledge is applied to simulate human brain functions, models abound on the evolution and advancements of machine translation tools and applications. This technology-driven turn alone has spawned evolving theoretical models ranging from rule-based architectures in the early days to statistics-based models in the second generation, and now the generation of neural network models constitutes the mainstream.

In order to get a better picture of interpreting studies in the last three decades and its development as an interdisciplinary study, we conducted a bibliometric study through CiteSpace, with data retrieved from Scopus to cover a wide variety of document formats, including journal articles, book chapters, books, and special issues of journals. The findings (see Figure 1) seem to suggest that, besides the terms directly linked with interpreting, interpretation, and translation such as "simultaneous interpreting," "interpretation ethics," and "sight translation," other co-occurring terms include "cognitive load," "working memory," "eye-tracking," "bilingualism," "multilingualism," and "language," suggesting the increasing multidisciplinary nature of interpreting research in recent years (Alves and Jakobsen, 2021; Ferreira and Schwieter, 2023).

Concerning the ten keywords with the strongest citation bursts in interpreting studies (see Figure 2), "multilingualism" (3.49, starting from 2015), "cognitive load" (4.22, starting from 2012), "eye-tracking" (3.65, starting from 2009), "refugee" (3.69, starting from 2020), and "sight translation" (4.6, starting from 2004) have registered the highest strength among the ten keywords. Among

Figure 1 Co-occurring keywords network of interpreting, generated by
CiteSpace in October 2022

Top 10 Keywords with the Strongest Citation Bursts

Keywords	Year	Strength	Begin	End	1993 - 2022
accreditation	2008	2.88	2008	2010	
community interpreting	2004	3.14	2012	2015	
interpretation	2001	2.83	2012	2014	
intercultural mediation	2013	4.2	2013	2014	
multilingualism	2015	3.49	2015	2016	
dialogue interpreting	2004	3.6	2018	2019	
sight translation	2004	4.6	2019	2022	
eye tracking	2009	3.65	2019	2022	
cognitive load	2012	4.22	2020	2022	
refugee	2020	3.69	2020	2022	

Figure 2 Top ten keywords with the strongest citation bursts, generated by
CiteSpace in October 2022

those, "sight translation," "eye-tracking," "cognitive load," and "refugee" have
shown their rapid citation bursts in recent years. Again, such broadening
perspectives as indicated in these bibliometric findings are being adopted and

pursued in current interpreting research at all levels. As we will argue, the field needs a comprehensive framework incorporating the internal (e.g., cognitive load, working memory, etc.) and external (e.g., ideological and sociocultural contexts, etc.) factors underpinning interpreting as a meaning-making process.

All of the theoretical perspectives and models mentioned are still relevant nowadays. They continue to provide constant inspiration to researchers and practitioners who subscribe to these distinctively articulated research paradigms by applying research methods typical of each tradition. As a whole, these well-defined perspectives have made significant contributions to our current understanding of the translating and interpreting process. Notwithstanding these contributions, these "turn"-driven perspectives, despite their unique contributions, still fall short of providing a unified theoretical framework within which translating and interpreting aptitude or competence can be explained adequately and predicted accurately as a highly complex social-cognitive activity that is situated and embodied within the external environment and the broader social-cultural context. In fact, in a situated interpreting activity, the sociological, cognitive, neurological, and technological elements are all unified in the interpreter in their professional practice, intensively reflected in determined moments and spaces (external social spaces or internal mental space) for the meaning-making of communications. In Pöchhacker's (2022) study, new forms of technology-based interpreting are discussed and seen to challenge deeply rooted assumptions about interpreting as a task. In human monitoring and postediting operations, with the machine performing the interlingual task and the human agent working interlingually, a more user-friendly version can be created, even for interpreting products. According to the author,

> Multi- or monolingual, the interpreters performing such intermodal intralingual tasks are still human beings, though the nature of their work, and hence their social and professional role, would be redefined: rather than foregrounding the real-time processing of two different languages, interpreters would be conceived as providing real-time access services which allow specific target users to overcome barriers to communication, be they linguistic, cultural, cognitive or sensory. (Pöchhacker, 2022: 159)

From this technological perspective, though the role of human agents will undergo a drastic shift from their original role as immediate agents between languages, the machine's intervention has made the multimodal and multilinguistic operation of interpreting an obvious showcase in both temporal and spatial senses.

Thus, we still need a unified theory that is comprehensive enough to succinctly encapsulate all the agents/stakeholders involved and the interplaying factors and elements of the translating and interpreting activity in multilinguistic and multicultural environments that are often superdiverse. Furthermore, such a unified theory should be able to capture the fluid, dynamic interactions between the translator/interpreter and all other essential internal and external factors alongside the multiple timescales (before, during, and after) of the translating and interpreting process. In this sense, it is fair to say that current theoretical models of these turn-oriented perspectives remain sporadic, fragmented, individual pieces of the full picture of the translating and interpreting aptitude puzzle. That is to say, the translating and interpreting field still needs a grand theory that not only portrays the nature and the architecture of translating and interpreting aptitude but also explains and predicts its dynamic dimensions of emergence, development, and real-time performance.

To resolve most, if not all, of these issues, we believe that with the advent of the translanguaging concept some thirty years ago in Welsh revitalization education programs (Williams, 1994, 2002), translanguaging theory has gradually emerged and been transformed into a practical and powerful theory explaining broad domains of human cognition and communication phenomena spanning the humanities and social sciences and beyond (Li, 2011a, 2018; Li and Zhu, 2013). Translating and interpreting, as multilingual-mediated communicative and social-cognitive activities, are constantly realizing translanguaging between and beyond different linguistic structures and systems. By the same token, translating and interpreting as viewed through this translanguaging lens cover the full range of linguistic performance by multilingual language users, who are transcending the combination of structures, the alternation between systems, the transmission of information, as well as the representation of values, identities, and relationships. Given the intricate entanglements between translation/interpreting and translanguaging (Baynham and Lee, 2019; Runcieman, 2021), we posit that it is now time for the field of translating and interpreting to construct a grand theory as a viable solution to a complete theoretical paradigm.

To this end, we endeavor to incorporate and integrate emerging insights from key tenets of translanguaging theory (Li, 2018; Li and Shen, 2021) into an aptitude model of translating and interpreting, with a view to explaining and predicting the emergence and development of the translation/interpreting process and to capturing the fluid and dynamic interactions between internal and external factors that are contributing to or exerting constraints on real-time performance and the final products of interpreting (see also Han et al., 2023).

3 Interpreting as Translanguaging: Rationale and Theoretical Foundation

As a well-established concept, translanguaging has emerged, evolved, and gradually been transformed as a practical and powerful theory of language communication and cognition (Li, 2011a, 2016, 2018, 2022). This theory has recently been argued and advocated by Li (2022) as a methodology offering a new conceptual framework that promotes a number of important analytical shifts and prompts us to ask different research questions and to find alternative ways of thinking and talking about data and methods of data collection and analysis. At its core, the translanguaging approach aptly captures and transcends the complex, dynamic, embodied, and adaptive interactions between human cognition (i.e., multicompetence) and the superdiverse social-cultural milieu. Since the turn of the century we have witnessed exponential growth and ubiquitous permeation of this new translanguaging lens being applied in a broad range of superdiverse phenomena and lived realities across the domains of humanities and social sciences. In lieu of these developments, the translanguaging approach has also provided methodological resources and countless inspiration for analyzing linguistic and artistic creativity and criticality in translingual practices embracing the multisensory, multimodal, multisemiotic, and multilingual nature of human communication as a meaning-making process (Li, 2016). Such an approach emphasize the spur-of-the-moment actions that can be treated as significant data points in understanding the rhythm and meaning of social life (Li, 2022).

Inspired by this methodological rationale, we also conducted bibliometric research through CiteSpace, with data retrieved from Scopus to find the co-occurring keywords network of "translanguaging" in the years since 2010. Scopus attempts to cover a wide variety of document formats (journal articles, book chapters, books, journal special issues, and journals). The bibliographic findings (see Figure 3) illustrate its frequency of co-occurrence with "multilingualism" (158), "bilingualism" (67), "bilingual education" (55), "codeswitching" (42), "language ideology" (39), "multilingual education" (37), "plurilingualism" (35), "multimodality" (32), "higher education" (32), "identity" (31), "language policy" (29), "teacher education" (28), "emergent bilingual" (24), "pedagogy" (24), "multilingual" (22), "English medium instruction" (21), "bilingual" (20), "translanguaging pedagogy" (19), "translation|" (18), "language" (17), "literacy" (17), "language education" (16), "linguistic repertoire" (16), "social justice" (16), "minority language" (14), "English" (14), "classroom discourse" (14), "biliteracy" (13), "language learning" (12), "superdiversity" (12), and "attitude" (12), among others, as shown in Figure 3. As we can see from this list, although "translation" is not

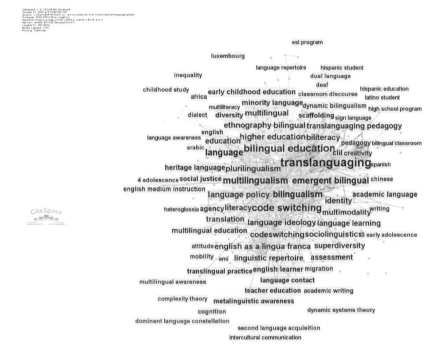

Figure 3 Co-occurring keywords network of translanguaging generated by CiteSpace in October 2022

among the most frequently co-occurring terms, as an activity that mediates human cognition and communication, it has made inroads into translanguaging academia and scholarly work.

3.1 What Is Translanguaging Theory and Why Is It Important for Constructing an Aptitude Model of Translating and Interpreting?

Translanguaging as a theory of human cognition and communication has gathered enormous momentum that permeates and transcends linguistic and disciplinary boundaries within a broad range of academic domains in humanities, social sciences, and beyond (Lee, 2021). As Baynham and Lee (2019: 24) have pointed out, translanguaging is "the creative selection and combination of communication modes (verbal, visual, gestural, and embodied) available in a speaker's repertoire." In essence, translanguaging theory captures the complex, dynamic, situated/embodied, and adaptive interactions between human cognition and the superdiverse sociocultural milieu. Since its inception in the 1990s (Williams, 1994), translanguaging theory has thrived, with exponential growth in the publication of books and papers applying the model in these broad domains. These domains have included but are not limited to bilingual and multilingual education, pedagogical and classroom instruction, language policy and planning, arts and literature, business and legal genres, urban city spaces, and sports (Han, Wen and Li, 2023; Li and Shen, 2021).

Perceived this way, translanguaging practices are situated and locally occasioned, being influenced and shaped by not just the immediate linguistic contexts but also the external tools/aids and technological affordances via multiple communication modes and multimodal means (cf. Baynham and Lee, 2019). Under this translanguaging lens, the implicated "languages" are no longer bounded entities but are typically conceived in the sense of "equitable multilingualism" (Ortega, 2019), in which purist monolingual models and benchmarks are discarded while bilingual or multilingual language ideologies are favored and adopted.

Baynham and Lee (2019) further presented the theoretical underpinnings of both translanguaging and translation and illustrated how translanguaging facilitates translation in everyday practice as well as in aesthetic works. Inspired by the concept of "translanguaging moment" (Li, 2011a) at which multilinguals creatively and critically translanguage to achieve specific communicative effects, Baynham and Lee (2019: 4, 182, 183) describe the "translation moments" as an assemblage with various resources available to the translator in the dynamic translation process. As such, they take translation as a trope and argue that the lens of translanguaging best captures the fluid and flexible practices of multilingual speakers who go between and beyond the language boundaries, not restricted to linguistic crossing, but making full use of the available "repertoire" for meaning-making, especially for the cases of untranslatability (e.g., Han, 2022).

Through this lens of translanguaging in translation studies, we now direct our attention to the translating and interpreting process, which can be conceptualized as a social-cognitive activity that implicates a bi/multilingual individual translator/interpreter engaging in successive translanguaging "moments" of meaning-making. Such a translanguaging practice naturally implicates the translators/ interpreters' multilinguistic repertoires (L1, L2, and Lx proficiency) and cognitive capacities (e.g., working memory, attentional control) interacting with the external environment and sociocultural contexts in which their attitudes, beliefs, and ideologies also play a part in affecting their translating/interpreting behavior and performance. Such complex interactions among the interplaying elements give rise to "translanguaging moments," spawning multilayered "translanguaging spaces" (Baynham and Lee, 2019):

> Translation can therefore be seen as embedded within a translanguaging space,
> at the same time as it is composed of successive translanguaging moments.
> This scalar view, best demonstrated in interpreting and think-aloud-protocols in

> translation, enables us to think of translation and translanguaging as being mutually embedded, such that we can speak of translation-in-translanguaging and translanguaging-in-translation. (p. 20)

By the same token, we can also argue that the two concepts of "translation-in-translanguaging" and "translanguaging-in-translation" proposed by Baynham and Lee (2019) can be further expanded and augmented by "translating/interpreting in translanguaging" and "translanguaging in translating/interpreting." In essence, the practice of translating/interpreting can now be regarded as the "fluid, dynamic, and multiple interchanges of repertoires and resources" in that:

> In superdiverse and translanguaging societies, source and target languages are no longer a one-to-one linguistic and cultural translation, but far more fluid, dynamic, and multiple interchanges of repertoires and resources that people access in multi-varied and multi-functional ways. (Runcieman, 2021, p. 1)

Runcieman further highlights the lens of translanguaging for pedagogy in interpreting:

> How could we start designing task-based curricula in interpreting studies to mirror potentially complex translanguaging scenarios? An approach that draws on plurilingual task-based exercises (Carreres et al. 2018; Cummins and Early 2014; González-Davies 2004), may be adapted to interpreting activities in the classroom (Runcieman, 2021: 12) . . . There is undoubtedly much more research required into developing effective didactic models, but this might be a starting point. (Runcieman, 2021: 14)

In short, the situated and embodied contexts and environment surrounding the agent of the translator/interpreter during the practice of translating and interpreting are congruent with the key tenets and principles of translanguaging theory. In the multilayered translanguaging space, the translator/interpreter makes full play of their multilingual, multimodal, and multisemiotic repertoire, selecting elements that do not necessarily have to be linguistic to illustrate how the visual, the verbal, the disembodied, and the embodied resources contribute to the orchestration of meaning of communication. At the successive translanguaging moments, a variety of cognitive, semiotic, and modal resources are dynamically mobilized and interact among themselves during the translating/interpreting process, aiming for a fluid and meaningful performance. As such, we postulate that translanguaging theory represents an ideal theoretical framework to conceptualize the practice of translating and interpreting. By applying the key tenets of the theory, we now turn to construct the aptitude model of translating and interpreting and specify its putative components or factors to capture the dynamic interactions of the interlocking elements that are at play while the translating and interpreting practice is undertaken by the agent of translation and interpretation within the superdiverse sociocultural environment.

Overall, we argue that such a translanguaging lens for interpreting, when augmented by integrated research methods from neighboring disciplines, such as the dynamic systems approach, allows us to adequately simulate, explain, and predict the emergence, real-time performance, and developmental trajectories of interpreting. The 3M Model has significant theoretical and methodological implications for future inquiries into translation and interpreting studies and practice.

To further delineate the key tenets of translanguaging theory and to evaluate its potential contributions to translation and interpreting practice, we are building a unified theory of translation and interpreting aptitude that portrays the nature and contexts of the translation and interpreting process to succinctly capture the dynamic interactions among the implicated agents and stakeholders within the superdiverse multilingual, multicultural, multisemiotic social and linguistic environment. Above all, we argue that multilayered "translanguaging spaces" (Li, 2011a) permeate the translation and interpreting process and products as a result of the successive moments of "translation and interpreting in translanguaging" and "translanguaging in translation and interpreting."

As a "snapshot or crystallization of a theory" (Setton, 2015: 263), the 3M Model aims to simulate, predict, and explain the translation and interpreting process, products, and functions by gleaning insights from the key tenets of translanguaging theory. As shown in Figure 4, the 3M Model is schematically mapped to three levels (or domains), along with its social-cognitive and linguistic repertoires (stock of speech styles, registers, varieties, and languages) (cf. Coulmas, 2005/2013; Spolsky, 1998) of putative translanguaging spaces, namely, either "translation and interpreting in translanguaging" or "translanguaging in translation and interpreting." We will next elaborate on putative factors and elements comprising each level to depict their key features and relational interactions (see Figure 5).

(1) The Micro Level – The Multicompetent Translator/Interpreter

The micro level of the 3M Model represents the translator/interpreter's most inner cognitive and mental activities or tasks as viewed under the microscopic lens of translanguaging. At this level, the key feature is the translator/interpreter's "multicompetence" (Cook, 2016), namely all of the cognitive and mental capacities and processes the translator/interpreter brings to bear on the translation and interpreting behavior and performance. The translator/interpreter's multicompetence at this level manifests itself during the essential skills and processes that are involved in the translating/interpreting stages. For example, being the most complex activity of interpreting, proceeding and succeeding in

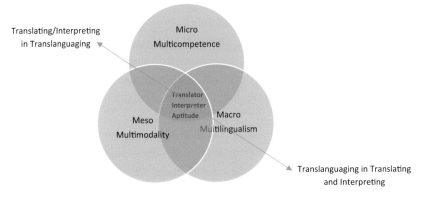

Figure 4 The schematic 3M Aptitude Model of translating and interpreting
(Han et al., 2023: 330)

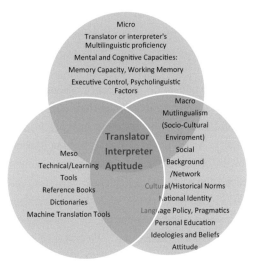

Figure 5 A fuller view of the 3M Aptitude Model of translation and interpreting
with indicative elements (Han et al., 2023: 338)

this task likely entails a heavy cognitive load or effort to be directed toward such
stages and processes.

(2) The Meso Level – Multimodal Affordances
The meso level of the 3M Model highlights the feature of multimodality that
aims to capture the dynamic interactions taking place between the translator/
interpreter' inner multicompetence (as described at the micro level) and the
externally available tools, aids, or technologies from the physical environment

(e.g., terminology, glossary, dictionary, computer-aided tools, machine translation software, or other aids). From these relations between the key agent (i.e., the translator/interpreter) and the tools and other multimodal and multisemiotic resources (i.e., external objects), we envision successive and iterative translanguaging moments of translation/interpreting that are distinct from those at the micro level.

(3) The Macro Level – Multilingual Society
The macro level of the 3M Model features the boundary-crossing dimensions of translating/interpreting in translanguaging as embodied and situated within the superdiverse multilingual sociocultural milieu. Within this societal context, influence from the ideological and language policies, the political and power relations between the agents and the vested stakeholders, identity issues, and meaning negotiations are ubiquitous, albeit covert. In the interactions among the engaging agents and the vested stakeholders (e.g., the translator/interpreter, the employer, the client, the editor/publisher, the readers, the audience, etc.), social constraints, cultural/historical norms (e.g., ideology, language policies), and national identity are key interplaying factors. Among these interactions taking place in the translanguaging spaces at this level, multilingual ideologies prevail over the purist monolingual or regulated bilingual language ideology (Baynham and Lee, 2019; Garcia and Li, 2014).

3.2 Further Considerations

To conclude this chapter, the translanguaging-informed 3M Model of translation and interpreting constructed here allows us to reconceptualize translation and interpreting aptitude more comprehensively and thoroughly. From this translanguaging lens, aptitude for translation and interpreting should be conceived as the blended or overlapping process of three defining properties nested within networks of indicative elements: (1) at the micro level, the person- or individual-based agency of multicompetence; (2) at the meso level, the tool-based or technology-driven affordances of the external environment; and (3) at the macro level, the social-politically normed multilingual ideologies. Theoretically, given its comprehensiveness, the 3M Model has perceivable advantages over previous level-specific or element-specific models to simulate or analyze certain aspects of the translation and interpreting process. More importantly, given its blending and overlapping portrayal, such a translanguaging-informed model allows us to capture adequately the complex, dynamic, and fluid interactions of the situated embodied processes that figure prominently in the successive translanguaging moments of meaning-making during translation/interpreting. Such a portrayal resonates well with the foundational theory of lexical concepts and cognitive models of Evans (2010) and the embodied simulation theory of Bergen (2012) in conceptualizing mechanisms of meaning-making that also underpin and transcend the translation and interpreting process and products.

Furthermore, the 3M Aptitude Model entails concerted efforts from multiple disciplines and integrated research methods spanning linguistics, sociology, ethnography, psychology, and other humanities and social sciences domains. To facilitate this, we highlight and recommend some potential research methods from the well-established approach of the complex dynamic systems theory (Hiver and Al-Hoorie, 2019; Holland, 2006; Larsen-Freeman and Cameron, 2008; Verspoor et al., 2011), as both translanguaging and dynamic systems theory approaches have much in common in "transcending disciplines" when probing the indicative elements influencing second-language acquisition and development (Hiver, Al-Hoorie and Larsen-Freeman, 2021; Larsen-Freeman, 2017) in which translating/interpreting skill plays an integral part (Wen, 2016 and 2021). Table 1 summarizes the three levels of the 3M Model alongside their embedded components and features, augmented by recommended research methods that can be adopted in future research. In this sense, we hope that the model will not just transcend and break down cognitive, social, and linguistic boundaries within the individual, but also transcend disciplinary boundaries,

Table 1 The 3M Translation and Interpreting Aptitude Model

Levels	Micro level (Multicompetence) (CDST-driven)	Meso level (Multimodality)	Macro level (Multilingualism)
The focus of Interactions with the translator/ interpreter	Linguistic competence Cognitive processes Executive control	External contexts Technological affordances	Superdiverse environment Sociocultural norms Identity
Examples	Basic linguistic knowledge and skills Basic cognitive abilities Memory capacities Attentional control Coordination	Tools and aids (e.g., dictionaries) Equipment and technologies (lab facilities, machine translation)	Cultural norms Social networks Group dynamics National identity Language policies Ideologies Attitudes Beliefs Pragmatics
Research methods Recommended	Think-aloud protocols Psychometric and cognitive testing, neurocognitive techniques (EEG, fMRI, etc.)	Classroom observation Audio-video recording; Questionnaires Surveys; Interviews Human versus machine translation comparison	Questionnaires Surveys Ethnographies Narrative analysis Social network analysis Corpus-based studies Computer modeling

achieving what Holmes (1988: 67, referring to Hagstrom) has called "disciplinary utopia" (also cited in Xiao and Muñoz, 2020).

Overall, we argue that such a translanguaging lens for interpreting, when augmented by integrated research methods from neighboring disciplines such as the dynamic systems approach, allows us to adequately simulate, explain, and predict the emergence, real-time performance, and developmental trajectories of interpreting. The 3M Model has significant theoretical and methodological implications for future inquiries into translation and interpreting studies and practice.

4 Translanguaging (Spaces) in Simultaneous and Consecutive Interpreting: Moment Analysis

Conference interpreting is a cognitively demanding activity that encompasses consecutive interpreting (CI) and simultaneous interpreting (SI). Increasingly, conference interpreting is no longer conceptualized simply as a linguistic rendering from one monolingual expression to another. Rather, it has been viewed more dynamically as a situated and embodied engagement of the bilinguals/ multilinguals transcending the two "worlds" to make meaning by resorting to multilingual, multimodal and multisemiotic repertoires. Viewed from the lens of translanguaging (Li, 2018), the interpreting process can be regarded as a highly complex and dynamic cognitive activity that implicates a bi/multilingual individual (i.e., the interpreter) engaging in successive "translanguaging moments" for meaning-making (Han et. al., 2023).

In the temporal sense, as immediacy marks the unique characteristic of interpreting that takes place in real-time (Pöchhacker, 2016, 2022), it makes time one of the conditioning dimensions of interpreting. As interpreting does not take place in a vacuum, the spatial and physical environment in which an interaction takes place and the agents involved in the interaction make space another conditioning dimension of interpreting. In the dimensional world with time and space weaving longitude and latitude, the interpreting activity is rather viewed as a situated and embodied engagement of the bilinguals/multilinguals transcending two spheres by resorting to multilingual, multimodal, and multisemiotic repertoires. The dynamics interwoven by time and space articulate the transformative power by addressing all the tensions and interactions in interpreting practices. When translanguaging is regarded as method (Li, 2022), this analytical point of view explores the temporal and spatial dimensions of interpreting. If we zoom in on the complex and rationalizing process of both consecutive interpreting (CI, via note-taking behaviors) and simultaneous interpreting (SI, through analysis of pauses) task engagement, we can further probe into the heart of the "translanguaging spaces" and the "spur of moments" in interpreting.

As such, the following study sets out to analyze the momentary complexity and dynamic architecture of the interpreting process by focusing on the distinct workflow tasks of SI and CI, with a view to better understand the underlying nonlinearity, emergence, and self-organization dynamics of these two interpreting modes. More importantly, we aim to advance current knowledge on interpreter engagement from a micro-level perspective as informed by the emerging theory of translanguaging in human cognition and communication (Li, 2018). We combined textual description with multimodal transcription to analyze interpreters' "translanguaging moments" during the SI and CI task performance. In particular, we video-taped and focused on the interpreters' note-taking and note-reading (specifically for CI), facial expressions, gestures, images, speech, and textual outputs during the interpreting process.

4.1 Translanguaging as Method

Space and time are two key concepts in translanguaging theory (Li, 2011a, 2011b, 2013, 2018, 2022). In the seminal article by Li (2011a), they are conceptualized in translanguaging theory as "translanguaging space" and "moment analysis".
Translanguaging space is defined as:

> a space for the act of translanguaging as well as a space created through translanguaging ... . The notion of translanguaging space embraces the concepts of creativity and criticality, which are fundamental but hitherto under-explored dimensions of multilingual practices. (Li, 2011a: 1222)

Further:

> Translanguaging spaces are not physical locations or historical contexts only, but are networks of social relations, real or virtual, that are created by individuals through distinctive (of the network) and shared (amongst the network members) practices for specific social purposes. ... It is worth repeating that translanguaging spaces are interactionally constructed. (Li, 2011a: 1225)

In the definition, space as "networks of social relations" is generated by translanguaging. The translanguaging space should be understood either in real or in virtual circumstances, embracing multilayered interactions that break down the ideologically laden dichotomies in "practices for specific social purpose". This definition is further elaborated as the translanguaging theory develops and extends its amplitude. The translanguaging space enables the act of translanguaging that goes between and beyond the different linguistic structures, cognitive and semiotic systems, and modalities (Li, 2018).

A translanguaging space has much to do with the vision of Thirdspace articulated by Soja (1996) as a space of extraordinary openness, a place of critical exchange where the geographical imagination can be expanded to encompass a multiplicity of perspectives that have heretofore been considered by the epistemological referees to be incompatible and uncombinable (Li, 2018: 23–24). This break-though "Thirdspace" view of translanguaging space embraces the multiplicity of perspectives, enabling an extraordinary openness to a multilingual, multimodal, and multisemiotic approach and methodology in research, unfolding multilayered perspectives in negotiation activities of meaning-making, with creative and critical elaborations of task engagement.

In light of the concept of translanguaging space, in the present section, our focus will be two-fold. On one hand, we emphasize the fluid and interchangeable space of interpreting, where the visual, audio, and body movements interact dynamically. On the other hand, we also focus on the mental working space of interpreting, where the eye movement, facial expressions, and gestures are intermingled in silent pauses, in terms of struggling efforts to summon together all the different resources of personal history, past experience, and the real-time contexts.

Regarding the dimension of time, Li defined the term "moment analysis" in task engagement from a temporal sense. According to him,

> A moment can be a point in or a period of time that has outstanding significance. It is characterized by its distinctiveness and impact on subsequent events or developments. People present at such moments would recognize their importance and may adjust their behavior according to their interpretation of them. Once it has occurred, a moment becomes a reference point or a frame; patterns can be detected by comparing the frequency and regularity of such moments. This definition of the moment is connected to Lefebvre's concept of rhythm in his rhythm analysis (e.g., 2004) which is concerned with various kinds of repetitions of actions of the human body and in daily life. But instead of measuring the intervals of repetitions, Moment Analysis focuses on the spur-of-the-moment actions, what prompted such actions, and the consequences of such moments including the reactions by other people. (Li, 2011a: 1224)

In Li's words, a moment, as "a point in or a period of time," is associated with time and sensitive to time. It is entailed in events or developments and frames the situated agents' behavior. As a concept similar to rhythm, a moment is related to "repetitions of actions of the human body and in daily life" and its dynamics in translanguaging lies in the "spur-of-the-moment actions," which, in its own terms, is called Moment Analysis.

Taking into account the definition of Moment Analysis, we select the situated moments in both modes of conference interpreting (CI and SI) for analysis. For CI, the situated note-taking/reading moments are chosen since they are considered as the reference points in rendering performance, showing the translanguaging dynamics with "spur-of-the-moment actions." The review of notes in conjunction with the interpreter's note-reading (rendition) allows for better inferences, which in return triangulates our understanding of the utility of notes. For SI, the pause moments are selected. They are part of the rendering, either silenced or filled, and constitute consequently "a period of time." During this duration of time, all silent/ filled but dynamically mobilized repertoires of the interpreter are in full preparation for the multimodal, multilinguistic, and multisemiotic "spur-of-the-moment actions."

4.2 Conference Interpreting: Translanguaging Spaces and Moments

Resorting to translanguaging as method, we extracted some close-ups of situated and embodied moments of the interpreting performance from an empirical study for analysis. The empirical study was designed and conducted among a group of students (from Portuguese to Chinese – Mandarin or Cantonese) whose CI and SI interpreting performance has been recorded. The performance was then transcribed and analyzed (see Figures 6 to 20). Close-ups of situated and embodied moments were analyzed based on the multimodal transcription of the SI and CI interpreting data. Note-taking/reading (for CI) and pauses (for SI) are the foci of analysis, where all the facial expressions, gestures, eye, and body movements, as well as other audio and visual elements are under consideration.

4.2.1 Situated Moments in CI and Its Translanguaging Space

Note-taking/reading is used as a means to organize the oral information of the original speech in a hierarchical way on paper (at the note-taking stage) and then from its written form to an organized oral rendition (at the reading stage) by recalling the information encoded in the notes. This practice conveys the oral-written-oral cycle, mixed with symbols, alinguals, abbreviations, and strokes, illustrating continuous behavior of interpreting with the intensive engagement of cognition. To get a comprehensive picture of the close-ups of note-taking/ reading, we chose three representative moments: the moment of note-taking/ reading a syntactically complex sentence, the moment of note-taking/reading a semantically complex sentence, and the moment of note-taking/reading a sentence with two figures. All these three types of moments present challenging cognitive tasks in the limited time of interpreting (problem recognition, solution proposal, and solution evaluation). During the tasks, besides the metric of ear–pen span (Chen, 2020) that measures the latency between a source language utterance and the start of a pen notation, it would be constructive to observe the cognitive constructs by describing, understanding, and explaining the multilingual, multimodal, multisemiotic, and multidimensional tensions and negotiations at the moments of note-taking/reading. As abbreviation and symbols in an interpreter's notes might be hypothesized as an indicator of language encoding and comprehension (Mellinger, 2022: 107), both abbreviation and symbols are to be analyzed to glean the interpreter's behavior and cognition, alongside the strokes and alingual notes (González, Vasquez, and Mikkelson, 2012) employed by the interpreter. With the two-layered moments of note-taking (reflected by notes) and reading (rendition moment reflected by close-ups of screenshots), we glean a better picture of the mental processing dynamics of the participants, as the latter triangulates the written data. Basically product-oriented, the multimodal description with notes and close-ups of screenshots provides a dimensional perspective to decipher the momentary cognition and behavior of participants. The original text in Portuguese (with English translation) and the multimodal description of the performance of each participant (interpretation transcription in Chinese, image of note-taking, and screenshot of the respective interpreting moment) are shown in the following examples.

Moment Analysis of CI in Note-Taking/Reading a Syntactically Complex Sentence

(a) Original speech in Portuguese (input): *Para assegurar o rendimento mínimo aos produtores as regras comunitárias, as regras da União Europeia, preveem que as organizações de produtores possam retirar do mercado os produtos da pesca que não atinjam determinado preço.*

English translation: To guarantee the minimum income for producers, the Community rules, the rules of the European Union, foresee that the producer organizations can withdraw from the market the fishery products that do not reach a certain price.

Analysis: This is a syntactically complex sentence with infinitive and subordinate sentences. Starting with the preposition *"para"* ("for" in English) to introduce an infinitive, this clause introduces its objective. This is one of the key pieces of information for interpreters to react and anticipate the following ideas. In this type of structure, the subject is key information and appears generally right after the infinitive. As this is an oral speech, there are naturally repetitions of ideas. In this long sentence, the subject is repeated twice: *"as regras comunitárias"* ("the community rules" in English) and *"as regras da União Europeia"* ("the European Union rules" in English). Generally, the interpreters' general knowledge could help them identify that it is a repetition rather than two different subjects so that they can relieve

Note-taking	Screenshot moments of note-reading

Figure 6 Multimodal description of Participant A

themselves of the semantical comprehension load and focus on reconstructing the sentence.

The following key information is led by "*preveem*" ("foresee" in English). This verb starts a subordinate clause that implies the use of the verbal conjunctive "*possam*" ("might" in English). With this anticipation, attention could be collocated in the functional verb "retirar" ("withdraw" in English) to grasp the essential information. In addition, in this clause there is another attributive clause that further complicates the clause structure – "*os produtos da pesca que não atinjam determinado preço*" ("fishery products that do not reach a certain price" in English). The multilayered structure increases interpreters' analytical effort and thus constitutes a difficult moment.

(b) Multimodal transcription of the performance of participants (interpretation transcription, note-taking, and screenshots of the moments of note-reading)

(1) Participant A (see Figure 6):
Rendition in Chinese (output): 那么为了能够保证中小生产者的最低收益, 欧盟就推出了一个决定, 那就是那一些捕捞上来的鱼类如果没有抵达一个最低的销售金额的话, 那么它们就会被回收。

Literal translation in English: In order to ensure the minimum income for small and medium producers, the EU has introduced a decision, that is, if the caught fish does not reach a minimum sale price, they will be recycled.

Analysis: The notes were simple, containing symbols (X, $), complete and shortened Portuguese words, as well as an abbreviation, and were well structured. Participant A read the notes and looked from time to time at the computer screen (the supposed public), with her hands holding the exact page of the notebook. Her performance was smooth and comfortable. Not influenced by the structural complexity, participant A succeeded in transforming the oral input into visualized symbols and abbreviations in a notebook and then by note-reading she reorganized and transformed the symbols and abbreviations into an oral production in the target language. Her mobilization of all the sensors (eyes, ears, hands, mouth) involved in the note-taking/reading moments construed multilayered translanguaging spaces, either physical or mental, culminating in multisemiotic and multimodal transcendence from one language to another. All the meanings of the symbols, abbreviations, and shortened words (EU, X, $) in the notes were correctly recalled and uttered in the target tongue, well organized with the contextual information, and, finally, resulted in an efficient performance.

(2) Participant B (see Figure 7):

Rendition in Chinese (output): 喺欧盟, 有, 有部分嘅渔获啦, 系被捕获到啦, 但系因为回收嘅价格系偏低, 所以渔民都唔同意去出售俾回收商。

Literal translation in English: In the EU, there is, there is some fish caught (la), caught (la), but because the recycling price is pretty low, fishermen wouldn't agree to sell fish to recyclers.

Analysis: The notes of Participant B had four shortened Portuguese words, one abbreviation (EU), two drawings (one is the circle that probably represents "recycle") and one symbol ($, meaning price). The notes presented condensed information about the complex ideas of the original speech. Seemingly informative,

Note-taking	Screenshot moments of note-reading
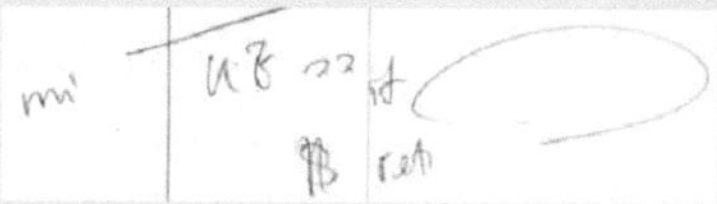	

Figure 7 Multimodal description of Participant B

the notes captured neither key verbs nor the structural logic. Participant B tried to find the missing messages from the glossary, by switching her looks from glossary to notes several times. This apparent nervousness led to her hesitation in performance, uttering unduly repeated words and the Cantonese modal particle "la," which added no substantial meaning but might gain her time to retrieve her memory for further information. In addition, Participant B made no eye contact with the computer screen (the supposed public), but shook the pen in her right hand. Her inner struggle was also externally observed by the uneasy eye movements, gestures, and disturbed utterances. In her case, the syntactically complicated structure of the source speech generated moments of intense cognitive tensions competing for resources. As a result, she tried to activate her other sensors (eyes, hands) to help to reconstruct memory and speech logic. These momentary efforts are shown in the close-up of a screenshot.

(3) Participant H (see Figure 8):
Rendition in Chinese (output): 一批海鲜嘞亦都会受到一*d*规矩去限制啦，例如佢哋嘅价钱嘞，亦都系受到控制嘅。

Literal translation in English: A batch of seafood (le) will also be restricted (la) by rules, such as their prices (le), which are also controlled (ge).

Analysis: The notes of Participant H were simple, containing two complete Portuguese words ("*regras*" meaning "rules" and "*obrigações*" meaning "obligations"), Chinese characters in full ("限制" meaning "restrictions"), and one symbol. As the complete words both in Portuguese and in Chinese require time and provide only limited information, he looked at the glossary and the notes alternately, trying to find additive information. He also looked at the screen,

Note-taking	Screenshot moments of note-reading
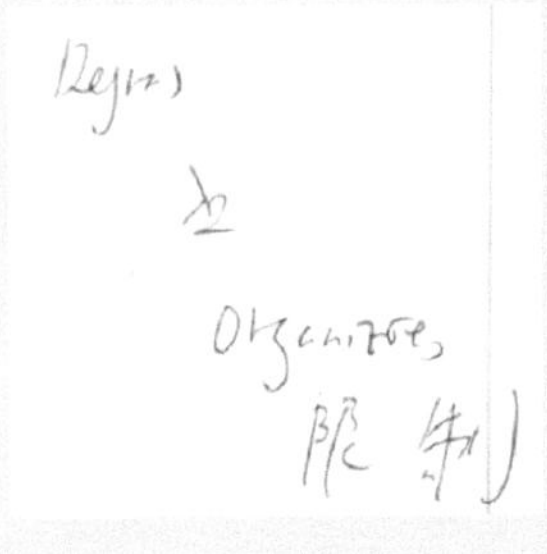	

Figure 8 Multimodal description of Participant H

trying to find other resources to relieve the uneasiness. The uneasiness was further reflected in his performance with the repetitive use of modal particles that were not semantically meaningful. He grasped the fragmented idea of the written words but failed to utter the inner logic. Though traces of translanguaging in his notes could help to mobilize his multilingual resources, the inner logic of these words was not regulated in memory. The mere reading of notes did not echo other cognitive resources to formulate non-linear dynamics. As a result, he failed to transmit the ideas.

Moment Analysis of CI in Note-Taking/Reading a Semantically Complex Sentence

(a) Original speech in Portuguese (input): *Este preço é denominado como preço de retirada comunitário e é definido anualmente pela Comissão para cada tipo de produto, portanto para peixe, para crustáceos, para mariscos em geral.*

English translation: This price is called the community withdrawal price and is defined annually by the Commission for each type of product, therefore, for fish, for crustaceans, for shellfish in general.

Analysis: Syntactically, this sentence is not complicated and not a long one. But in terms of information density, it presents difficulty. The first part of the sentence explains the name of the withdrawal price, which is the first key information. The second part explains who ("the Commission") sets the price and the frequency ("annually"). Right after that, there is a list of enumeration "fish, shellfish, crustaceans"). In the limited time, interpreters are required to analyze the information, manage their memory, and react in their notes with an almost simultaneous rhythm. In this case, with a heavy load of memory, visualization might be the best solution, together with several keywords or symbols.

(b) Multimodal transcription of the performance of participants (interpretation transcription, note-taking, and screenshots of the moments of note-reading)

(1) Participant A (see Figure 9):
Rendition in Chinese (output): 那么它们就会被回收，那这一些产品就包括鱼类啊，像是甲壳类的海产品，总之就是大多数的海鲜产品都会经过这一个项目。

Literal translation in English: Then they will be recycled, and these products include fish (a), such as crustacean seafood, in short, most seafood products will go through this project.

Note-taking	Screenshot moments of note-reading

Figure 9 Multimodal description of Participant A

Analysis: The notes of Participant A were written down in a translanguaging manner, where we can observe Chinese characters ("回收价" meaning "withdrawal price") and complete Portuguese words ("*peixe*" meaning "fish" and "*marisco*" meaning "seafood"). As the information was dense and she wrote little, she tried to find more information from the glossary, as well as from the computer screen. This nervousness was reflected in rendition. A modal particle "a" appeared in her interpreting when she turned to the glossary. Apparently, the modal particle was of no added substantial meaning for the performance but gained her time. Due to lack of simplified/fluid symbols to substitute the complete words, she showed some uneasiness by missing some information, but the uneasiness was instantly relieved when she mobilized personal interpreting experiences by organizing the sporadic elements in a logical way.

(2) Participant B (see Figure 10):
Rendition in Chinese (output): nil

Analysis: The notes of Participant B contained a symbol ($) and two Chinese characters ("訂", meaning "define" and "年", meaning "year"). At the note-reading, she omitted the information. It was observed that she was turning over the page with her pen in her right hand, her eyes fixing on the notes. No doubt, this omission showed her momentary broken articulation between memory and note-taking and no effective resources were mobilized to bridge the broken articulation.

(3) Participant H (see Figure 11):
Rendition in Chinese (output): nil

Analysis: Even though Participant H correctly wrote down key information of the original speech in complete Chinese and Portuguese words, complemented by

Note-taking	Screenshot moments of note-reading

Figure 10 Multimodal description of Participant B

Note-taking	Screenshot moments of note-reading
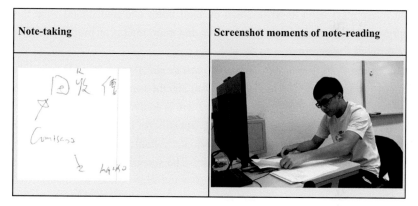	

Figure 11 Multimodal description of Participant H

arrows to indicate directions and relations, he omitted the whole information, showing neither pause nor hesitation in his delivery. He had a lot of eye contact with the virtual client (screen) in front, with one hand holding the pen and the other always preparing to turn the page. At the note-reading stage, he initiated a given-up strategy by focusing on other information he had much more confidence in. As a matter of fact, a well-structured and informative note-taking is constructive in memory retrieval, and the fact that participant H missed information reveals his weakness in coordinating all relevant cognitive constructs in a balanced way.

Moment Analysis of CI in Note-Taking/Reading a Sentence with Two Figures

(a) Original speech (input) in Portuguese: *Após este processo, cabe às mais de mil instituições de solidariedade social, apoiadas pelos bancos alimentares, distribuir os cabazes pelas mais de 200 mil pessoas que recebem este tipo de apoio.*

English translation: After this process, more than a thousand social solidarity institutions will distribute, under the support of food banks, baskets to more than 200 thousand persons who receive this type of support.

Analysis: As we know, numbers have been considered one difficulty for interpreters. Numbers for Chinese/Portuguese interpreters are no exception, as the two languages have completely different numerical systems. Chinese numerical units advance every four digits after 10,000 while Portuguese numerical units advance every three digits after 1,000. So the conversion between these two languages requires not only memory but also cognitive effort. Besides, numbers are not meaningless digits but represent dense information behind every number. In consecutive interpretation, numbers are information that interpreters need to write down on their notes and understand what they represent. Unlike some logical arguments that interpreters can predict, numbers are difficult for interpreters to foresee.

In this example, there are two figures: "*mais de mil*" ("more than a thousand" in English) and "*mais de 200 mil*" ("more than 200 thousand" in English). The first one is relatively less problematic because there is equivalence in Chinese and no conversion of numerical units is required. But still, for interpreters to note down what the number represents "*instituições de solidariedade social*" meaning "social solitary institutions") can be tricky. The second figure is a big number and requires the interpreter to convert to 20 wan (wan=10,000) in Chinese.

(b) Multimodal transcription of the performance of participants (interpretation transcription, note-takings and screenshots of the moments of note-reading)

(1) Participant A (see Figure 12):
Rendition in Chinese (output): 随后将会，通过超过*1,000*个慈善组织将这一些鱼类分发给超过*20*万的正在经历饥饿和贫困的人。

Literal translation in English: After that, more than 1,000 charity organizations will distribute the fish to over 200,000 persons who are experiencing hunger and poverty.

Analysis: Participant A showed the figures correctly on her notes in their abbreviation forms. The notes contained shortened Chinese characters, English abbreviations, mathematical symbols, and Portuguese words. "k" was used to represent one thousand in this case. In the notes, it was observed that multi-linguistic and multisemiotic symbols were mobilized to construct memory. At the note-reading stage, she said correctly the two figures and the information about the figures. In addition, she retrieved all the memory from the note and delivered

Note-taking	Screenshot moments of note-reading
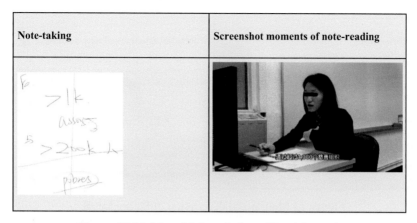	

Figure 12 Multimodal description of Participant A

a fluent and smooth performance. This confident performance was also manifested by her natural and steady eye contact with the virtual client (screen).

(2) Participant B (see Figure 13):

Rendition in Chinese (output): 一d位于唔同地方嘅粮食银行啦, 嘅目嘅数
字系达到*1,000*家嘅, 咁, 呢一个计划由最初生生效到依家啦, 已经系有*20*
万人系接受到呢一个帮助。

Literal translation in English: Some food banks are located in different places
(la), and the number, the number of them reaches 1,000 (ge). Well, from the
beginning of this plan to now (la), 200,000 persons have already received this help)

The notes of Participant B showed correct figures, with fragmented contextual information. She used Chinese characters, Portuguese words, and symbols
in a mixed way to register the information. For example, the symbol "m" in her
notes represented "*mil*" ("thousand" in English). She had informative notes and
correctly delivered the two figures. However, she was so stuck to the written
information that she omitted other related modifying components, which made
her imprisoned by the notes at the note-reading stage. This entanglement was
evidenced by her note-reading performance: she used the pen to point out every
word she was interpreting. In addition, when interpreting the information
related to the figure "200,000," she frowned and inappropriately repeated
words, which revealed inner conflicts and uncertainty. Though in her note-
taking she resorted to the translanguaging method, at the note-reading stage
she failed to retrieve the diverse cognitive constructs in memory, failing to
mobilize all available resources (due to cognitive constraints) to formulate
positive dynamics.

Note-taking	Screenshot moments of note-reading

Figure 13 Multimodal description of Participant B

Note-taking	Screenshot moments of note-reading

Figure 14 Multimodal description of Participant H

(3) Participant H (see Figure 14):

Rendition in Chinese (output): 然后就由食物银行将呢批海鲜交到去有需要嘅人身上, 咁根据呃上年嘅数字呢个计划嘞就可以将食物传送到去20万人手中。

Literary translation in English: After that, the food bank will deliver the batch of seafood to those in need. Then according to (ge) the figures of last year, this plan (le) can deliver the food to 200,000 persons.

Analysis: The notes of Participant H showed his confusion about numbers. He paid very close attention to the figure "200,000," with the figure being written three times in the notes. Each time with different symbols: one Arabic number, one combination of an Arabic number and a Portuguese word, and the third a combination of an Arabic number and a Chinese character. When interpreting the content with the figure "200,000," the participant paused briefly and looked at the glossary, trying to identify the figure and remember the original message behind the figure. Since he spent a lot of time on this number, he didn't mention the other figure. Also, he invented information alien to the original speech, which, fortunately, did not lead his delivery in the wrong direction. This deviation showed once more the internal entanglement of cognitive resources, while the great potential of memory had not yet been developed into resourceful dynamics due to the unbalanced distribution of cognitive constructs.

Summary

With the multimodal transcription and description of the challenging moments in terms of cognition of interpreters at the CI stage (moments of note-taking and reading of a structurally complex sentences, of a semantically complex sentence, and of a sentence with numbers), we can approximate some inspiring findings from a translanguaging perspective. The translanguaging-informed moment analysis of note-taking and note-reading provides an innovative method to predict and eventually evaluate interpreting quality, which is usually analyzed through interpreting performance and delivery (product). The entangling moments in note-taking, reading, and coordination of cognitive constructs manifest the dynamic interactions among languages, sensory input, and cognition during the interpreting process. By describing, analyzing, and explaining these challenging moments, we see the inner struggle and uneasiness when the resources available are unbalanced distributed, like the switching looks (eye movements) from glossary to notes. We also see the confident and fluent delivery when all the linguistic, semiotic, and sensory repertoires are mobilized, like the note-reading aided by reinforced memory. We further see undue invention that deviates from the speech when the cognitive efforts are wrongly allocated. In all, the tensions and negotiations of all the resources involved in the CI activity are either overtly reflected by eye movements, gestures, and linguistic hesitations with a lot of modal particles, or covertly manifested by information deviation, omission of information, and imprisonment by notes. Though the method of translanguaging has been more or less used in note-taking, it has not yet been fully developed at the stage of note-reading together with other cognitive apparatus like memory. Even Participant A whose performance is good shows her hesitance and uneasiness when facing semantically dense sentences. To break through the bottleneck, translanguaging continues to be a methodological apparatus, which helps to liberate further our constraints from notes, by resorting to our memory and cognitive potentials. This translanguaging underpinning of note-taking/reading recognizes the situated nature of interpreting and probes into embodied and distributed cognition.

4.2.2 Constrained Moments in SI and Its Translanguaging Space

In the highly time-sensitive SI, the temporal immediacy shows the competition of the entire cognitive load, when the input verbal information is visualized and archived in the mental space, processed simultaneously with newly input verbal information, and then verbally rendered in another language. As shown by many SI studies, the whole process tolerates a time lag of between two to five seconds; otherwise, the accuracy is considerably endangered (Barik, 1973; Lee, 2002). The time lag can serve as a temporal variable and sensitive measure to reflect the speed of underlying processing in the cognitive approach to research on interpreting (Timarová, 2015; Timarová et al., 2011). As "pauses are interruptions in the flow of speech" (Mead, 2015: 332), pause detection and analyses have been used as a means of time lag in both translation and interpreting studies (Butterworth 1980; Dragsted and Hansen, 2009; Han and An, 2021; Jakobsen 1998). As an observable variable, a pause can visibly show the hesitation and boundaries between the verbal input and verbal output in SI and help visualize the complex moments of competition of cognitive load semiotically. With this rationale, we applied pause analysis as a measure of time sensitivity in analyzing the SI task and focused on the pauses in this study that lasted longer than five seconds (the maximum tolerance temporal length).

For the experiment, the preliminary analysis shows the common pauses are mainly associated with two types of sentences of the original utterance that show structural or semantical complexity. We selected two sentences for detailed analysis: sentence 1 is an adverbial clause (led by "*o que* ... "), which is syntactically complex and long; sentence 2 is complex in terms of content (with numbers and a list of names). We use the same translanguaging method in the pause analysis of SI, by analyzing the multimodal performance of some representative participants of the experiment. We continue to study the same three cases as we do in CI analysis. Though Participant A showed no pause length over five seconds, her case still served for us to understand other pause cases. For the second sentence, considering the similarity between cases B and H, we substitute case B with case D to make our analysis more representative. The original text (with English translation) and the description of the performance of each participant (interpretation transcription, pause occurrence in the video, and the screenshot of the respective moment) are shown as follows:

Pause Analysis of SI Closeups of a Structurally Complex Sentence

(a) Original input in Portuguese: ... *o que aparentemente nem sequer corresponde a uma verdade absoluta já que o facto de haver um elemento físico ancorado no mar, faz com que haja uma tendência para que os seres* *marinhos se agreguem à volta dessa zona, portanto, aumentando provavelmente também a possibilidade de haver peixe para pescar.*

English translation: … which apparently does not even correspond to an absolute truth, because having a physical thing anchored in the sea makes marine beings aggregate around that area, which, therefore, probably increases the possibility of having fish to catch.

(b) Multimodal transcription of the performance of participants (interpretation transcription, pause occurrences in the video, and screenshots of pause moments)

(1) Participant A (see Figure 15)

Rendition in Chinese (output): 因为毕竟它是一个在海中建立的一系列的建筑群所以说对于海洋动物来说也是有影响的.

Literal translation in English: Because after all, it is a series of buildings established in the sea, it also has an impact on marine animals.

Analysis: Participant A, though she did not show any pauses more than five seconds long, demonstrated uneasiness in other aspects. There is no doubt that the structural complexity challenged her competence to its limits. She resorted to the glossary, moved her hands, and made gestures, trying to find relief from the stressful situation. Apparently, this mobilization of available resources had positive effects. Though the delivery was not precisely the original information, the information transmitted was not deviation, but

Pause occurrence in the video	Screenshot of pause moments (of the first 5 seconds)
N/A	

Figure 15 Multimodal description of Participant A

Pause occurrence in the video	Screenshot of pause moments (of the first 5 seconds)
07:34-07:40	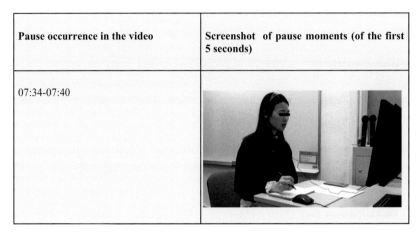

Figure 16 Multimodal description of Participant B

something vague and similar to the original idea, which enabled her to survive the crisis.

(2) Participant B (see Figure 16)
Rendition in Chinese (output): 因为海洋嘅生物会离开一个树立咗风车嘅地方.

Literal translation in English: Because marine creatures will leave a place ("ge") where a windmill is erected.

Analysis: During participant B's pause (six seconds), she stared at the screen, looking around at times, frowning. She held a pen firmly but noted down nothing. The information she reproduced was contrary to the meaning of the original speech. Her delivery did not render the basic idea and she failed to understand the original information. During the pause, she tried to control her uneasiness, but her frown revealed her dissatisfaction with her performance and her inner struggle. She did not recall the information in time and her other sensory resources were not effectively mobilized in coordination with information chunking.

(3) Participant H (see Figure 17)
Rendition in Chinese (output): Nil.

Analysis: Though Participant H paused for six seconds, he produced nothing at the end of the pause. Obviously, he had difficulty understanding the information, but he tried to reinforce sensory input by pressing continuously the

Pause occurrence in the video	Screenshot of pause moments (of the first 5 seconds)
09:21-09:27	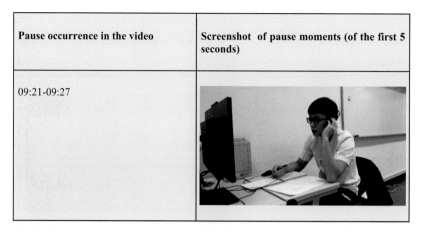

Figure 17 Multimodal description of Participant H

headset. At the same time, he blinked several times at the screen, adjusting body positions and moving his lips silently. These minor actions showed his efforts to activate memory and other sensorial constructs, though nothing was finally produced. The whole information was omitted. The strong pressure exerted by SI was vividly presented in this performance.

Pause Analysis of SI Closeups of a Semantical Complex Sentence

(a) Original speech (input) in Portuguese: *A maioria dos parques eólicos marítimos estão, encontram-se em zonas pouco profundas e a pelo menos 2 kms da costa, em geral estarão a uma média de 5 kms da costa. Estão também distantes das rotas marítimas, das zonas militares, das zonas de interesse natural ou das rotas de migração das aves.*

English translation: Most offshore wind parks are located in remote areas and at least 2 kms from the coast. Generally they will be at an average of 5 kms from the coast. They are also far away from sea routes, from military areas, from areas of natural interest or from bird migration routes.

(b) Multimodal transcription of the performance of participants (interpretation transcription, pause occurrences in the video, and screenshots of pause moments)

(1) Participant A (see Figure 18):
Rendition in Chinese (output): 这要求至少有2,000米的海洋线或者是5,000米同样都要离军事基地又或者是自然保护区和鸟类迁徙的主要途径要避免这一些地方.

Pause occurrence in the video	Screenshot of pause moments (of the first 5 seconds)
N/A	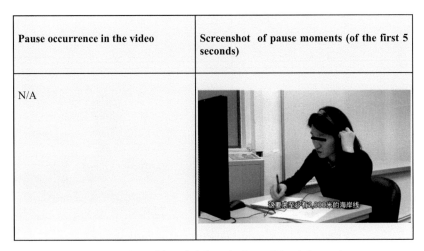

Figure 18 Multimodal description of Participant A

Literal translation in English: This requires at least 2,000 meters of sea line or 5,000 meters away from military bases or nature reserves and the main route of bird migration. These places should be avoided.

Analysis: Participant A took notes of numbers and glanced at the glossary for terminology support. Without any pause of over 5 seconds, she processed the information in a timely manner. Though she looked around and frowned when attempting to resolve potential problems, her rendition was fluent, with one hand resting on the headset. Her interpretation correctly reproduced both figures as well as almost all the terminology. Her efforts to mobilize memory (via note-taking, for numbers) and available resources (glossary for terms) gained her cognitive efficiency and resulted in a workable performance. Her self-organization was reinforced by her excellent linguistic proficiency in comprehension and oral production.

(2) Participant D (see Figure 19):
Rendition in Chinese (output): 大部分的海洋上建立的风力发电站一般是离海岸2到5米2到5公里的距离一般来说要远离那些鸟群迁徙的路径.

Literal translation in English: Most of the wind power plants built on the ocean are generally 2 to 5 meters away from the coast, and the distance of 2 to 5 kilometers is generally away from the route of those birds that migrate.

Analysis: Participant D had three consecutive long pauses. At the first pause (eight seconds), the participant blinked continuously with one hand pressing the

Pause occurrence in the video	Screenshot of pause moments (of the first 5 seconds)
1. 04:37-04:45 2. 04:49-04:55 3. 05:01-05:08	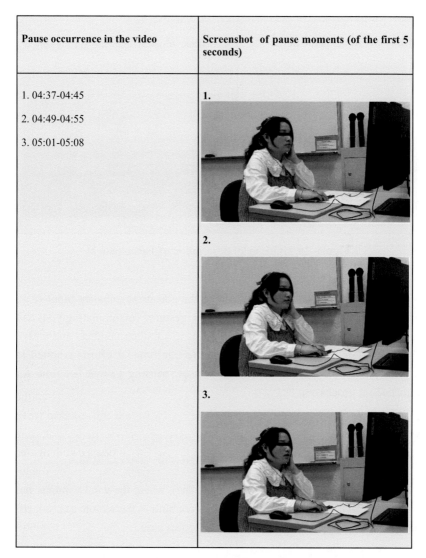

Figure 19 Multimodal Description of Participant D

headset, and the other hand manipulating a pen, looking at the screen. The information she produced was pertinent and correct. During the second pause (six seconds), when processing the information related to the figures, the participant moved her lips, as if simulating speech. Then she uttered the right numbers twice. The first time she uttered the wrong units but the second time with the right number of units. For the third pause (seven seconds), she blinked continuously and played with the pen on the table while staring at the screen. She also succeeded in producing the right term. Considered as three mini-consecutive

Pause occurrence in the video	Screenshot of pause moments (of the first 5 seconds)
05:48-05:55	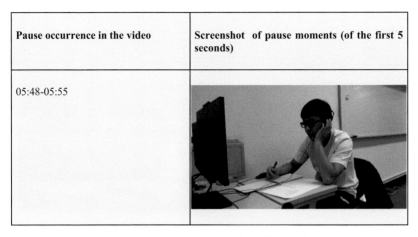

Figure 20 Multimodal description of Participant H

interpretings, Participant D made use of the pauses to enhance input (e.g., pressing headset), to mobilize resources by gestures (manipulating pen) and reinforce her memory (e.g., moving her lips to simulate numbers and units). Though the delivery was less cohesive, her multimodal efforts resulted in a positive performance. In these three cases, pausing gained her time for information processing.

(3) Participant H (see Figure 20):

Rendition in Chinese (output): 咁通常呢 *d* 风力风力发电站嘅 *d* 风车会建喺边度嘞就系起喺远海地区啦咁亦都唔系一 *d* 一带一路经过嘅地方.

Literal translation in English: So usually (ne), where the wind windmills of the wind power station are built (le)? They are built at the remote sea (la), but not the places by which the Belt and Road routes pass.

Analysis: During Participant H's pause (seven seconds), his eyes never left the screen, with one hand pressing the headset and the other playing with a pen. He also moved his lips as if simulating speech. By adding modal particles in his delivery, he tried to gain time for more information. He missed key information and concrete numbers, but he tried to make a summary of the complex ideas. Though this effort was laudable, unfortunately, the information summarized was far from the original idea. The final information ("Belt and Road" routes) was invented information, not related to the original speech. Though his cognitive resources (e.g., analytical capacity) during a very limited time were mobilized, the lack of linguistic repertoire was still a big handicap for Participant H.

Summary

In summary, the SI pause analysis has shown us another illuminating perspective to study the time sensitivity entailed in interpreting. In the pause analysis, the silences are full of meaning. When probing into the pauses, we see behind the pause the internal struggles and searches in the linguistic, cognitive, and semiotic resources of the participants. The pause can indicate a blackout for someone or a space of analysis for others. The apparent blackout is a confusing moment when all the resources are struggling for position chaotically, when self-organization has failed to generate meaning-making renditions; however, as self-organization is an ongoing mental process, the continuous boundary-breaking employment of resources contributes to emergence dynamics. All the entanglements are happening in a nonlinear order. We notice that excellent linguistic proficiency in comprehension and production consumes less cognitive effort and releases more resources, which helps to improve the dynamics greatly, as shown by Participant A. Contrary to the case of Participant A, Participant H failed in several tasks. not due to his lack of mobilization of resources, but due to his relatively weak linguistic repertoire. A promising example is Participant D, who has shown us how she mobilizes her available resources to make the impossible possible.

4.3 Conclusion and Future Implications

Based on the different time-sensitivity of CI and SI, the empirical study examines the momentary complexity and dynamic architecture of the distinct workflow tasks of the two modes of interpreting within the working definition of translanguaging and its key tenets. Through the analytical lens of "moment analysis" advocated by translanguaging theorists (Li, 2011a; also see Lee, 2022), this section has explored the temporal and spatial interpreting by zooming in on the complex and rationalizing process of both CI (via note-taking behaviors) and SI (through analysis of pauses) task engagement, to further probe into the heart of the "translanguaging spaces" in interpreting. As amply demonstrated by the foci on the interpreters engaging in the tasks, during the situated moments of CI, the activities involved in the note-taking and note-reading, including the visual, audio, and body movements, were all mobilized and coordinated in a fluid and interchangeable space. On the other hand, during the constrained moments of SI, which were manifested externally as silent "pauses," all the eye movements, facial expressions, and gestures revealed the interpreters' mental tension and their struggling efforts to summon together different resources of personal history, past experience, and the real-time contexts, collectively contributing to creating a mental working space. This micro-level perspective of both the note-taking/reading (CI) and pause (SI) analysis underpin the underlying nonlinearity, emergence, and self-organization dynamics of listening comprehension, production, and the ear–voice span between the hearing of the source speech and its corresponding reformulation.

In the same vein, through these situated and constrained moments, we discern the eye and body movements, facial expressions, and gestures as well as other audio and visual markers, in interaction with language comprehension and production in interpreting. These "visible embodiments" of cognitive processing in consecutive and simultaneous interpreting demonstrate that conference interpreting practice is not restricted to auditory perception and oral production, but is a multidimensional, complex, multimodal, and rationalizing activity. As the mental and cognitive tasks accumulate, the internal dynamics assemble, unite, and mobilize all the available repertoires of one's cognition, aptitude, and sensors. Though apparently seen as multitasking, the intense struggle and interaction of the cognitive constructs under the tasks of CI and SI are hidden beneath the "visible embodiments" for orchestration of meaning-making. Overall, we argue that, under the powerful magnifying translanguaging lens, all close-up scenarios of the CI and SI moments are interwoven in the time and space dimensions, affording the interpreters the transformative power to make meaning that communicates. The results and findings of the empirical study reported here further corroborate that simultaneous interpreting and consecutive interpreting entail different levels of time sensitivity and likely consume different amounts of cognitive resources within the translanguaging environments. As such, it is hoped that the present study serves as a good starting point to find better solutions in interpreting studies that will orient the interpreting students' coping strategies in attentional allocation and control, both in CI and in SI.

5 Translanguaging in Community/Public-Service Interpreting

5.1 Historical contextualisation of Community/Public-Service Interpreting

The role of the interpreter has deep historical roots, going back to ancient civilizations (Baigorri-Jalón, 2015), although the emergence of interpreting as a modern-day profession came about only relatively recently, in the 1950s and 1960s. Its first professional recognition was in the field of "conference interpreting" in the wake of the Second World War with the need to establish simultaneous[3] court interpreting at the Nuremberg Nazi war crime trials, where English, German, Russian, and French were the principal languages of

---

[3] Simultaneous interpreting refers to the interpreter's shadowing of the interlocutor, principally through wireless receivers involving headphones and microphones, interpreting/reformulating their speech at the same time as they are speaking. This is different from consecutive interpreting, where the interpreter waits for the speaker to pause before interpreting their speech to the other party/parties.

the court. Later, in 1953, the Association Internationale d'Interprètes de Conférences (AIIC) [International Association of Conference Interpreters] was established to represent and protect the rights of professional conference interpreters, and in 1969 this association went on to forge agreements with the UN and the Council of Europe with regard to relevant training, accreditation, and acceptable remuneration for its members (García-Beyaert, 2015).

"Community interpreting" emerged later, principally in the 1970s in Australia (Chesher, 1997), initially to represent the linguistic and cultural rights of aboriginal communities, and subsequently in Canada[4] to address the same in the country's French enclaves (i.e., Quebec). This professional field then spread to America and the EU in the 1980s, principally in response to the successive waves of immigration during and after the Second World War and the need to manage interlingual/intercultural communications between the public institutions of host nations and their increasing multilingual and multicultural communities. Although community interpreting became firmly established as a term from then onwards (Pöchhacker, 1999), another, "public-service interpreting," also emerged in the 1990s in the UK, with the creation of the Diploma in Public Service Interpreting (DPSI) by the Chartered Institute of Linguists, in conjunction with the Nuffield Foundation, revising the syllabus in the Certificate in Community Interpreting (CCI) "to reflect more closely the changing needs of people using or working with 2 or more languages in the public services" (Hammond, 2007: 1). Public-Service interpreting has many sectors, which have seen a certain degree of interpreter specialization; for example, court/legal interpreting, healthcare interpreting, and social services interpreting.

Despite existing for over fifty years, however, community/public-service interpreting[5] still remains relatively unrecognized internationally as a profession (D'Hayer, 2012). Whereas some countries have accredited bodies to certify and promote it, such as Canada, America, Australia, and *some* European countries like the UK and Austria (D'Hayer, 2012; Mikkelson, 2014; Ozolins, 2014), others, such as Portugal, persist in treating it as an ad hoc service that can be carried out by untrained (semi)bilinguals (D'Hayer, 2012). Moreover, even in those countries that do recognize it as a profession, there is still an uneven form of standardization, varying in terms of curricula in higher education and professional training institutions (De Pedro Ricoy, 2010) and variations in course duration, methodology, core pedagogic principles, assessment processes, and quality control (D'Hayer, 2012).

---

[4] Although it has always been referred to there as "cultural interpretation."

[5] We use both terms from here on to capture the interrelation between the two and to suggest that when one term is used it is inevitably related to the other, although this is perhaps not explicitly stated.

Community/public-service interpreting is very different from conference interpreting in that conference interpreting is more concerned, broadly speaking, with remote simultaneous interpreting of monological speech, where interpreters sit in booths with headsets and microphones to relay talks on specific subjects that they have already prepared for (i.e., technical language, subject-specific terms and expressions, etc.). Community/public-service interpreting on the other hand is usually a presential[6] and dialogical interaction (see Wadensjö, 1998) between the interpreter and two or more parties, often with diverse sociolinguistic and sociocultural interlocutors (Angelelli, 2006).

5.2 Relevance of Translanguaging to Community/Public-Service Interpreting

The community/public-service interpreter is closely impacted by the emergence of translanguaging practices in the community as they are principally concerned with interpreting between the organs and institutions of the state and immigrant communities (inter alia, in education, healthcare, and legal settings), working potentially therefore with the very people who might translanguage in their daily lives (Runcieman, 2022), those people who draw on all their resources to "get things done" (Pennycook and Otsuji, 2015). This occurs not only in their public lives but also in their parochial and private lives as well, where, for example, multilingual/multicultural families navigate their social lives in complex interlingual/intercultural ways (Creese, Blackledge and Hu 2018).

As community/public-service interpreting has nearly always been framed as an interchange between Language A (LA), representing the majority language of the state, and Language B (LB), the minority language of the immigrant community (Runcieman, 2021), this raises serious issues about how to cope with instances of translanguaging and how interpreter training curricula need to address the phenomenon.

An example of how translanguaging is intricately tied to an individual's process of knowledge construction and lived experience can be found in Runcieman's (2022) research into court interpreting, a branch of community/public-service interpreting. Based on a discourse analysis of interviews with six professional court interpreters in the UK, instances of translanguaging were shown to have regularly emerged in court cases. For example, in one instance that emerged in the research, a Polish–English interpreter reports how he was talking to his Polish client in their shared primary language, Polish, when the client introduced lexis that was based on English verbs and nouns but adapted to Polish morphosyntactic structures: "***Skin****owałem **chickeny***" (I was skinning chickens); "Rozmawiałem

---

[6] Although much more through video since the COVID-19 pandemic (see Runcieman, 2021).

z ***supervisorem***" (I was talking with the supervisor); "*Byłem* na ***kitchen****ie*" (I was working the kitchens). Runcieman's analysis showed how:

> (i)n these examples, English verbs and nouns have undergone a form of translanguaging. In the first example, the English verb "to skin" has taken the Polish suffix *-owałem*, indicating the past-imperfect aspect (i.e., "I was skinning"). The object of the verb, "chickens," .... is given the Polish plural suffix *-ie*, represented here by the letter *-y* (with the same phonemic value, /i:/, in both languages): *chickeny*. The next two examples show the English noun "supervisor" being given the *-em* suffix to signal an instrumental noun in Polish and "kitchen" again taking a Polish plural /i:/ phoneme, represented by an alternative orthographic representation *-ie*. (Runcieman, 2022: 12)

The research argued that although the English lexis used was readily available in the client's primary language (confirmed by the interpreter), the client's experiences of a potentially unfamiliar form of employment (i.e., skinning chickens) in an English-speaking labor market had become an essential means of communicating about it, *even* to a fellow Polish speaker. The client's knowledge construction of his new occupation and his experience in the English labor market had forged a translanguaged form of expressing it. Moreover, it was argued that far from being just a "broken" "work-related lingo," as the interpreter described it, it did in actual fact show consistencies in structure, a creative, translanguaging, linguistic melding of the unfamiliar (i.e., skinning chickens in the English labor market) with the familiar (i.e., Polish grammar; for a description of the research and a fine-grained analysis of the data, see Runcieman, 2022).

5.3 New Routes in Interpreter Training: Accommodating Translanguaging

Curricula in interpreting studies have long followed monolingual ideologies in their pedagogy (Runcieman, 2021), particularly in the persistent monolingual approach to teaching language acquisition in general, where practices such as codeswitching are generally considered as deficit (Li, 2016). However, these ideologies are being increasingly challenged by an approach to applied practice seen through a translanguaging lens. In the following, we highlight how some of these major changes are emerging in the field.

Specifically related to translation studies,[7] translanguaging approaches are already being introduced in task-based activities and curricula (see Carreres et al., 2018; Cummins and Early, 2014; González-Davies, 2004). González-Davies' research has focused on how multilingual texts can be

---

[7] Translation studies, is admittedly different from interpreting but related in its objective of linguistically and culturally transmitting content from one semiotic system to another.

navigated by participants outside the scope of their assigned linguistic competencies and indeed further their multilingual and multicultural competences in general by sharing their semiotic resources through a process of sociocultural "scaffolding", drawing on and sharing all their semiotic resources and mediating meaning through group discussion and consensus.

Specifically, in the field of interpreting, "conference interpreting" research has begun to explore how translanguaging can enrich conference events. O'Connor and colleagues (2022) have researched how actively encouraging and promoting trilingual translanguaging affected their 14th Inter-American Symposium on Ethnography and Education as it took place over three days on both sides of the US–Mexico border (with English, Spanish, and Portuguese speaking participants). Here, organizers, keynote speakers, and attendees were all actively encouraged to communicate in whatever language they preferred without concerns about monolingual-bounded restrictions, ultimately, the researchers/organizers claimed, enriching the event (O'Connor et al., 2022).

Specifically, in the field of community/public-service interpreting, Runcieman (2021) has proposed introducing a "translanguaging space" (drawing on Li, 2011a) in interpreting curricula:

> This space might be a classroom discussion on the challenges to professional interpreting practice in a translanguaging world, where students, through teacher-student interaction, could share their ideas about best practices, as well as explore their emerging social and professional identities in this context . . . Post-modernist discourses on the relationship between minority and majority language groups could also be addressed and explored, as well as how globalization and neoliberalism have played their part in this re-evaluation. (Runcieman, 2021: 143)

Drawing on González-Davies' work in translation, Runcieman (2021) has also proposed a practical, task-based activity, to initiate research into future ways of developing students' multilingual and multicultural competencies from a translanguaging perspective. Drawing on role play, an omnipresent classroom exercise in interpreter training globally, he has suggested taking a non-monolingual approach (e.g., LA–LB, English–Spanish, etc.) by introducing translanguaging into a pre-recorded (video) example of a multilingual exchange to stimulate students to draw on all their linguistic repertoire in order to prepare them for their future professional careers, where translanguaging could undoubtedly be a possibility among their clients. This pre-prepared video exercise outlined a potential step-by-step set of activities, based on the following potential scenario:

> A French surgeon, who spent five years specializing in Germany, has been working in a Spanish hospital for over three years. His Spanish corresponds to a C1 level in the CEFR.

He needs to communicate with an English-speaking patient in the presence of his Spanish colleagues, to discuss the probable outcomes of an operation, engaging the services of a Spanish–English interpreter.

At certain points in his speech he is unable to express specific information and/or socio-cultural expressions in Spanish and uses alternatively French and German words and phrases, pausing as he realizes these might be incomprehensible to his interlocutor and/or interpreter.

At each instance where this happens the video will be paused, and working in groups, students will summarize the content in the target language (i.e., English) and explore the potential meaning of what was translanguaged in the discourse context. They will be given a time limit before the video is restarted (e.g., 5 minutes).

At the end of the video students will share their ideas about what was translanguaging, in the target language, and the reason for their choices.

Follow-up activities will involve a teacher–student debate on potential best practices when translanguaging occurs in interpreting, with an exploration of ethical considerations. (Runcieman, 2021: 146–47)

Although a very *euro-centric* and *profession-based* approach (focusing on European languages in a professional medical interaction), Runcieman suggested that future curricula development could draw more from the local demographic of the interpreter-student, their local languages (i.e., Urdu, Hindi, Cantonese, Mandarin, as well as dialects and/or regional variations) and diverse sociocultural perspectives. Moreover, other forms of community/public-service interpreting could be addressed, with more complex sociocultural and socio-economic dimensions, such as in asylum seeker and/or police interviews.

Another approach might be introducing what García and Lin (2017) refer to as the "three strands of translanguaging pedagogy" into interpreter training: a "translanguaging positioning and stance," a "translanguaging design," and a "translanguaging shift." A translanguaging positioning and stance are based on inducting teachers into the concept that all their students' bi/multilingual repertoires are "valid, authentic and important" (Garcia and Lin, 2017). This entails aiding teachers in challenging monolingual approaches and understanding that student assessment needs to be holistic, taking into account all their multilingual and multimodal means of expression simultaneously, critically, and reflectively, in their meaning-making processes, and designing their curriculum appropriately. Moreover, teachers need to be flexible, allowing for a shift in focus based on their students' questioning and potential (re)framing of their learning processes in a dynamic and continually emerging process (Garcia and Lin, 2017).

There are other more practice-based approaches that might also be considered, such as utilizing examples of translanguaging from interpreting corpora (i.e., court interpreting, and EU parliamentary interpreting, etc.) to explore how specific instances were navigated by the interpreter and discussing ethical dimensions and approaches to best practice.

5.4 Concluding Remarks

There is an urgent need for community/public-service interpreting studies to address the emergence of translanguaging practices that challenge territorial, monolingual approaches to language and culture. The geopolitical borders of nations are increasingly less representative of exclusive monolingual, monocultural worlds, although persistent dominant discourses and ideologies continue to pervade, based more on nationalistic, sociopolitical *will* than the realities on the ground (Li, 2018; Runcieman, 2022). Indeed, even more than in the past, one of the central *official* requisites for a migrant's assimilation into a host nation is their ability to speak the "national language" – "using and being tested in the standard language of the new country is not only a proxy for national unity but is a sine qua non of integration and social cohesion" (Simpson and Cooke, 2017: 6). In the UK, for example:

> Prior to 2002, there were no specific requirements to show evidence of suitability for settlement through a language test or a test of knowledge of society. Today, people applying for settlement are required to pass an English language examination at level B1 on the CEFR[8] in addition to the Life in the UK citizenship test. (Simpson and Cooke, 2017: 6)

Despite this sociopolitically imposed conflation of language and nationality, however, *Language* is becoming less and less the purview of the dictates of individual states (which propagate the concept that there is a *plurality* of *bounded* and *discrete* linguistic entities), and more and more, through a translanguaging lens, as rather a borderless shared reservoir of semiotic resources and affordances that can be, and are, drawn upon depending on the situated, spatiotemporal context of the communicative act in superdiverse societies (Li, 2018).

Translanguaging has already emerged in community/public-service interpreting (see Angermeyer, 2015; Runcieman, 2022). Indeed, further research will undoubtedly reveal its much wider impact in general. A major concern now though, is how interpreter pedagogies will rise to the challenge of language as no longer being a simple LA–LB interchange, but rather as an increasingly untethered, *deterritorialized*, and universal resource (Runcieman, 2021).

---

[8] The Council of Europe's Common European Framework of Reference for Languages tests language learners'/ users' competence in a foreign language on a scale ranging from A1 (Beginner) to C2 (Full proficiency). See www.coe.int/en/web/common-european-framework-reference-languages.

Translanguaging has emerged as an academic paradigm that has already begun to claim its "turn" in most of the language sciences: (bi)literacy studies, where it has its roots, ethnography, sociolinguistics, applied linguistics, and, it is argued here, more recently in translation and interpreting studies.

Regardless of the disciplines that are incorporating translanguaging into their gravitational pull though, we emphasize here that translanguaging is first and foremost a *practice*, part of urban multilingual/multicultural intercommunal communication in increasingly superdiverse societies in the late twentieth and early twenty-first centuries. Although there are other taxonomies, with subtly different approaches in the academy (i.e., polylanguaging, flexible bilingualism, metrolingualism, etc.), translanguaging differentiates itself by a certain set of specific foci with regard to pedagogy (albeit not without some inevitable cross-fertilization). Drawing from already observable and recorded translanguaging practices in educational settings (i.e., student–student, and teacher–student bi-/multilingual interactions) it seeks to shape educational policy "to maximize the students' and the teachers' full linguistic, cognitive, semiotic and socio-cultural resources in knowledge construction" (Li, 2017: 3) and their overall "communicative potential" (García, 2009: 140). Moreover, translanguaging embraces the *critical* and *creative* potential it has to free individual thought and expression from the limitations of monolingual bias (García and Li, 2014).

Translanguaging faces many "post-multilingual challenges" however (Li, 2016). The ties between individual languages and national identity are still substantive, as socioculturally ingrained and sociopolitically promoted convergences, as well as the threat of the *other* (language/culture), where *named* languages are conflated with ideologies of shared cultural beliefs, belonging, and unity that is potentially undermined by others. However, it is argued here, these are not insurmountable obstacles to change and can perhaps be eventually accommodated in future visions of superdiverse societies and an increasing sociopolitical acknowledgment of a translanguaging *reality* within individual nation-states that enriches rather than depletes the social and cultural world of its population (Runcieman, in press).

Interpreter training curricula need to introduce a "translanguaging space" and practical task-based exercises (see Runcieman, 2021), to understand how monolingual approaches to interpreting are increasingly being undermined and why, and to develop strategies for coping with this eventuality. Persistent monolingual approaches to language learning and practice are detrimental to the service that interpreters need to provide, a service that requires the interpreter to engage with the linguistic divergences that are emerging *naturally* in our continually evolving superdiverse societies globally.

6 Conclusion and Future Directions

Looking to the future then, a translanguaging research agenda for translation and interpreting studies can be expected to help frame and guide research towards more specific directions, theoretically and methodological couched within the "translanguaging turn" in translation/interpreting theory, research, and practice. For example, future studies can be designed to investigate these interplaying indicative elements at each, or all, of the three depicted levels proposed in the integrated framework here (i.e., the macro, the meso, or the micro level).

Also, given the interdisciplinary perspective adopted by the aptitude model (see Section 4), we call for synergetic cooperation and collaborations among scholars to make concerted efforts from different domains of translation/interpreting studies. Through these multidisciplinary endeavors, insights can be gleaned from such neighboring disciplines as sociology and cultural studies, linguistics, applied linguistics, bilingualism, education, psychology, cognitive science, computer science, and neuroscience to arrive at a deeper understanding of the interplaying factors underpinning the most complex cognitive activity of interpreting.

No doubt, the essence of the translanguaging theory lies in its flexibility, dynamics, adaptiveness, inclusiveness, and openness in breaking down cognitive, societal, linguistic, semiotic, and technological boundaries and artificial divisions and dichotomies (such as the social-cognitive divide [Atkinson, 2011; Douglas Fir Group, 2016; Hult, 2019]; the quantitative-qualitative divide [Hiver, Al-Hoorie, and Larsen-Freeman, 2021]). Such a translanguaging view is congruent with the current mainstream trends of multilingual societies of superdiversity, multiculturality, and multisemiotics (Ortega, 2019). We cannot wait to embrace this new and exciting translanguaging era in translation and interpreting studies (Baynham and Lee, 2019; Runcieman, 2021; Wen, Runcieman and Han, 2023).

Finally, we would also like to recommend some references for further reading. These include core readings for translanguaging both as a practical theory (Li, 2018) and as method (Li, 2022). Regarding research methodology, as argued by Lee (2022) and demonstrated in this Element, moment analysis has great potential for investigating the cognitive aspects of interpreting as translanguaging. In terms of the relationship between translanguaging and interpreting, we recommend readers also get more inspiration from Baynham and Lee (2019), Runcieman (2021), and Han, Wen, Lin and Li (2023). Finally, we strongly encourage our readers to read relevant literature from all other related fields, such as cognitive translation and interpreting studies and complex dynamic systems (e.g., Alves and Jakobsen, 2021; Dong, 2018; Schwieter and Ferreira, 2017; Schwieter and Wen, 2022). As we have demonstrated in this Element, interpreting as translanguaging is a multidisciplinary enterprise. As such, it requires multidisciplinary efforts.

References

Alexieva, B. (1997). A typology of interpreter-mediated events. *The Translator*, *3*(2), 153–174.

Alves, F. (2003). *Triangulating Translation: Perspectives in Process Oriented Research*. Amsterdam: John Benjamins.

Alves, F., and Jakobsen, A. L. (Eds.). (2021). *The Routledge Handbook of Translation and Cognition*. Abingdon: Routledge.

Androutsopoulos, J., and Juffermans, K. (2014). Digital language practices in superdiversity: Introduction. *Discourse, Context and Media*, *3*(4–5), 1–6.

Angelelli, C. V. (2006). Validating professional standards and codes: Challenges and opportunities. *Interpreting*, *8*(2), 175–193.

Angermeyer, P. S. (2015). *Speak English or What? Codeswitching and Interpreter Use in New York City Courts* (Oxford Studies in Language and Law). New York: Oxford University Press.

Appadurai, A. (1996). *Modernity at Large: Cultural Dimensions of Globalization*. Minneapolis: University of Minnesota Press.

Atkinson, D. (2011). A sociocognitive approach to second language acquisition: How mind, body, and world work together in learning additional languages. In D. Atkinson (Ed.), *Alternative Approaches to Second Language Acquisition* (pp. 155–178). Abingdon: Routledge.

Baigorri-Jalón, J. (2015). The history of the interpreting profession. In Mikkelson, H., and Jourdenais, R. (Eds.), *The Routledge Handbook of Interpreting* (pp. 11–24). London: Routledge.

Baker, C. (2003). Biliteracy and transliteracy in Wales: Language planning and the Welsh National Curriculum. In N. Hornberger (Ed.), *Continua of Biliteracy: An Ecological Framework for Educational Policy, Research and Practice in Multilingual Settings* (pp. 71–90). Clevedon: Multilingual Matters.

Barik, H. C. (1973). Simultaneous interpretation: Temporal and quantitative data. *Language and Speech*, *16*(3), 237–270.

Baynham, M., and Lee, T. K. (2019). *Translation and Translanguaging*. London: Routledge.

Becker, L. (1991). Language and languaging. *Language & Communication*, *11*(1–2), 33–35. https://doi.org/10.1016/0271-5309(91)90013-l.

Bergen, B. K. (2012). *Louder Than Words: The New Science of How the Mind Makes Meaning*. New York: Basic Books.

Butterworth, B. (1980). Evidence from pauses in speech. *Language Production*, *1*, 155–176.

Carreres, Á., Noriega-Sánchez, M., and Calduch, C. (2018). *Mundos en Palabras: Learning Advanced Spanish through Translation*. London: Routledge.

Chen, S. (2016). Note-taking in consecutive interpreting: A review with a special focus on Chinese and English literature. *The Journal of Specialised Translation, 26*(1), 151–171.

Chen, S. (2020). The process of note-taking in consecutive interpreting: A digital pen recording approach. *Interpreting, 22*(1), 117–139.

Chesher, T. (1997). Rhetoric and reality: Two decades of community interpreting and translating in Australia. In S. E. Carr, R. P. Roberts, A. Dufour, and D. Steyn (Eds.), *The Critical Link: Interpreters in The Community* (pp. 277–292). Amsterdam: John Benjamins.

Cook, V. J. (1992). Evidence for multicompetence. *Language Learning, 42*(4), 557–591.

Cook, V. (2016). Premises of multi-competence. In V. Cook and Li W. (Eds.), *The Cambridge Handbook of Linguistic Multi-competence* (pp. 1–25). Cambridge: Cambridge University Press.

Coulmas, F. (2005/2013). *Sociolinguistics: The Study of Speakers' Choices*. Cambridge: Cambridge University Press.

Council of Europe (2020). *Common European Framework of Reference for Languages: Learning, Teaching, Assessment – Companion Volume*. Strasbourg: Council of Europe Publishing. https://rm.coe.int/common-euro pean-framework-of-reference-for-languages-learning-teaching/16809ea0d4.

Creese, A., Blackledge, A., and Hu, R. (2018). Translanguaging and translation: The construction of social difference across city spaces. *International Journal of Bilingual Education and Bilingualism, 21*(7), 841–852.

Cummins, J. (1979). Cognitive/academic language proficiency, linguistic inter-dependence, the optimum age question and some other matters. *Working Papers on Bilingualism, 19*, 121–129.

Cummins, J., and Early, M. (2014). *Big Ideas for Expanding Minds*. Toronto: Pearson Education Canada.

De Pedro Ricoy, R. (2010). Training public service interpreters in the UK: A fine balancing act. *The Journal of Specialised Translation, 14*, 100–120.

D'Hayer, D. (2012). Public service interpreting and translation: Moving towards a (virtual) community of practice. *Meta, 57*(1), 235–247.

Dong, Y. (2018). Complex dynamic systems in students of interpreting training. *Translation and Interpreting Studies, 13*(2), 185–207.

Douglas Fir Group (2016). A transdisciplinary framework for SLA in a multilingual world. *Modern Language Journal, 100*, 19–47.

Dragsted, B., and Hansen, I. (2009). Exploring translation and interpreting hybrids: The case of sight translation. *Meta: Journal des Traducteurs/ Meta: Translators' Journal, 54*(3), 588–604.

Esteve, O., and González-Davies, M. (2017). Estratègies de transferència interlingüística en l'aprenentatge de llengües addicionals: Un Enfocament Plurilingüe Integrador. In M. Pereña (Ed.), *Ensenyar i Aprendre Llengües en Un Model Educatiu Plurilingüe* (pp. 6–16). Barcelona: Horsori.

Evans, V. (2010). *How Words Mean: Lexical Concepts, Cognitive Models, and Meaning Construction*. Oxford: Oxford University Press.

Ferreira, A., and Schwieter, J. W. (Eds.) (2023). *The Routledge Handbook of Translation, Interpreting, and Bilingualism*. London: Routledge.

Ferreira, A., Schwieter, J. W., and Festman, J. (2020). Cognitive and neurocognitive effects from the unique bilingual experiences of interpreters. *Frontiers in Psychology, 11*, article 548755. http://doi.org/10.3389/fpsyg.2020.5487.

García, O. (2009). *Bilingual Education in the 21st Century*. Oxford: Wiley Blackwell.

García, O., and Kleifgen, J. A. (2019). Translanguaging and literacies. *Reading Research Quarterly, 55*(4), 553–571.

García, O., and Li, W. (2014). Translanguaging in education: Principles, implications and challenges. In O. García and W. Li (Eds.), *Translanguaging: Language, Bilingualism and Education* (pp. 119–135). London: Palgrave Pivot.

García, O., and Lin, A. (2017). Translanguaging and bilingual education. In O. García, A. Lin, and S. May (Eds.), *Bilingual and Multilingual Education* (pp. 117–130). Cham: Springer.

García-Beyaert, S. (2015). Key external players in the development of the interpreting profession. In H. Mikkelson and R. Jourdenais (Eds.), *The Routledge Handbook of Interpreting* (pp. 45–58). London: Routledge.

Gerver, D. (1976). Empirical studies of simultaneous interpretation: A review and a model. In R. Brislin (Ed.), *Translation: Applications and Research* (pp. 165–207). New York: Gardner Press.

Gile, D. (1985). Le modèle d'efforts et l'équilibre d'interprétation en interprétation simultanée. *Meta, 30*(1), 44–48.

Gile, D. (1995/2009). *Basic Concepts and Models for Interpreter and Translator Training*. Amsterdam: John Benjamins.

Goffman, E. (1981). *Forms of Talk*. Oxford: Blackwell.

González, R. D., Vasquez, V., and Mikkelson, H. (2012). *Fundamentals of Court Interpretation: Theory. Policy and Practice*. Durham, NC: Carolina Academic Press.

González-Davies, M. (2004). *Multiple Voices in the Translation Classroom*. Amsterdam: John Benjamins.

Grosjean, F. (1982). *Life with Two Languages: An Introduction to Bilingualism.* Cambridge, MA: Harvard University Press.

Hammond, J. (2007). *Preface of the Diploma in Public Service Interpreting Handbook.* London: Chartered Institute of Linguists Educational Trust.

Han, C., and An, K. (2021). Using unfilled pauses to measure (dis)fluency in English–Chinese consecutive interpreting: In search of an optimal pause threshold(s). *Perspectives*, *29*(6), 917–933.

Han, L. (2022). Meaning-making in the untranslatability: A translanguaging analysis of the film love after love. *Theory and Practice in Language Studies*, *12*(9), 1783–89.

Han, L., Wen, Z., Lin, Z. Y., and Li, W. (2023). An aptitude model for translation and interpreting: Insights from translanguaging theory. In Z. E. Wen, P. Skehan, and R. L. Sparks (Eds.), *Language Aptitude Theory and Practice* (pp. 324–351). Cambridge: Cambridge University Press.

Hawkins, M. R., and Mori, J. (2018). Considering "trans-"perspectives in language theories and practices. *Applied Linguistics*, *39*(1), 1–8.

Hiver, P., and Al-Hoorie, A. H. (2019). *Research Methods for Complexity Theory in Applied Linguistics.* Bristol: Multilingual Matters.

Hiver, P., Al-Hoorie, A. H., and Larsen-Freeman, D. (2021). Toward a transdisciplinary integration of research purposes and methods for Complex Dynamic Systems Theory: Beyond the quantitative–qualitative divide. *International Review of Applied Linguistics in Language Teaching*, *60*(1), 7–22.

Holland, J. H. (2006). Studying complex adaptive systems. *Journal of Systems Science and Complexity*, *19*, 1–8.

Holmes, J. S. (1972). The name and nature of translation studies. In J. S. Holmes (Ed.), *Translated! Papers on Literary Translation and Translation Studies* (pp. 67–80). Amsterdam: Rodopi.

Holmes, J. S. (1988). *Translated! Papers on Literary Translation and Translation Studies.* Amsterdam: Rodopi.

Hornberger, N. H. (1989). Continua of biliteracy. *Review of Educational Research*, *59*(3), 271–296.

Hult, F. M. (2019). Toward a unified theory of language development: The transdisciplinary nexus of cognitive and sociocultural perspectives on social activity. *Modern Language Journal*, *103*, 136–144.

Jakobsen, A. L. (1998). Logging time delay in translation. *LSP Texts and the Process of Translation*, *1*, 173–101.

Kramsch, C., and Zhang, L. (2018). *The Multilingual Instructor.* Oxford: Oxford University Press.

Larsen-Freeman, D. (2017). Complexity theory: The lessons continue. In L. Ortega and Z. Han (Eds.), *Complexity Theory and Language*

Development: In Celebration of Diane Larsen-Freeman (pp. 11–50). Amsterdam: John Benjamins.

Larsen-Freeman, D., and Cameron, L. (2008). *Complex Systems and Applied Linguistics*. Oxford: Oxford University Press.

Larson, M. L. (1984). *Meaning-Based Translation: A Guide to Cross–Language Equivalence*. New York: University Press of America.

Lee, T. H. (2002). Ear voice span in English into Korean simultaneous interpretation. *Meta: Journal des Traducteurs/Meta: Translators' Journal*, *47*(4), 596–606.

Lee, T. K. (2021). *The Routledge Handbook of Translation and the City*. New York: Routledge.

Lee, T. K. (2022). Moment as method. *Research Methods in Applied Linguistics*, *1*(3), 1–4.

Levý, J. (1967/2018). Translation as a decision process. In *To Honor Roman Jakobson: Essays on the Occasion of his Seventieth Birthday*, vol. 2 (pp. 1171–82). The Hague: Mouton.

Li, D., Lei, V. L. C., and He, Y. (Eds.) (2019). *Researching Cognitive Processes of Translation*. Singapore: Springer.

Li, W. (2011a). Moment analysis and translanguaging space: Discursive construction of identities by multilingual Chinese youth in Britain. *Journal of Pragmatics*, *43*(5), 1222–35.

Li, W. (2011b). Multilinguality, multimodality, and multicompetence: Code-and mode switching by minority ethnic children in complementary schools. *The Modern Language Journal*, *95*(3), 370–84.

Li, W. (2016). New Chinglish and the post-multilingualism challenge: Translanguaging ELF in China. *Journal of English as a Lingua Franca*, *5*(1), 1–25.

Li, W. (2018). Translanguaging as a practical theory of language. *Applied Linguistics*, *39*(1), 9–30.

Li, W. (2022). Translanguaging as method. *Research Methods in Applied Linguistics*, *1*(3), article 100026.

Li, W., and Shen, Q. (2021). Translanguaging: Origins, developments, and future directions. *Journal of Foreign Languages*, *44*(4), 2–14 (in Chinese).

Li, W., & Zhu, H. (2013). Translanguaging identities and ideologies: Creating transnational space through flexible multilingual practices amongst Chinese university students in the UK. *Applied Linguistics*, *34*(5), 516–35.

Maturana, H. R., and Varela, F. G. (1980). *Autopoiesis and Cognition: The Realization of the Living*. London: Reidel Publishing Company.

May, S. (Ed.) (2013). *The Multilingual Turn: Implications for SLA, TESOL, and Bilingual Education*. London: Routledge.

McAuliffe, M., and Triandafyllidou, A. (Eds.) (2021). *World Migration Report 2022*. Geneva: International Organization for Migration.

Mead, P. (2015). Pauses. In F. Pöchhacker (Ed.), *Routledge Encyclopedia of Interpreting Studies* (pp. 301–3). London: Routledge.

Meier, G. (2017). The multilingual turn as a critical movement in education: Assumptions, challenges and a need for reflection. *Applied Linguistics Review*, *8*(1), 131–61.

Meier, G., and Conteh, J. (2014). Conclusion: The multilingual turn in language education. In J. Conteh and G. Meier (Eds.), *The Multilingual Turn in Languages Education: Opportunities and Challenges* (pp. 292–99). Bristol: Multilingual Matters.

Mellinger, C. D. (2022). Cognitive behavior during consecutive interpreting: Describing the notetaking process. *Translation & Interpreting*, *14*(2), 103–19.

Mikkelson, H. M. (2014). Evolution of public service interpreter training in the US. *FITISPos International Journal*, *1*, 9–22.

Moser, B. (1978). Simultaneous interpretation: A hypothetical model and its practical application, In D. Gerver and H. W. Sinaiko (Eds.), *Language Interpretation and Communication (NATO Conference Series III): Human Factors* (pp. 353–68). New York: Plenum.

Muñoz Martín, R. (2010). On paradigms and cognitive translatology. In G. M. Shreve and E. Angelone (Eds.), *Translation and Cognition* (pp. 169–87). Amsterdam: John Benjamins.

O'Connor, B., Mortimer, K., Bartlett, L., et al. (2022). Cruzar fronteras em espaços acadêmicos: Transgressing "the limits of translanguaging." *Applied Linguistics Review*, *13*(2), 201–42.

Ortega, L. (2019). SLA and the study of equitable multilingualism. *The Modern Language Journal*, *103*, 23–38.

Ozolins, U. (2014). Descriptions of interpreting and their ethical consequences. *FITISPos International Journal*, *1*, 23–41.

Pennycook, A., and Otsuji, E. (2015). *Metrolingualism: Language in the City*. London: Routledge.

Pöchhacker, F. (2016). *Introducing Interpreting Studies*. London: Routledge.

Pöchhacker, F. (2022). Interpreters and interpreting: Shifting the balance? *The Translator*, *28*(2), 148–61.

Runcieman, A. (2021). Proposal for a "translanguaging space" in interpreting studies: Meeting the needs of a superdiverse and translanguaging world. *Translation and Translanguaging in Multilingual Contexts*, *7*(2): 133–52. https://doi.org/10.1075/ttmc.00070.run.

Runcieman, A. (2022). Translanguaging in court proceedings: How interpreter pedagogy needs to address monolingual ideologies in court interpreting which delegitimize litigants' voices. *International Journal of Interpreter Education, 14*(1), 17–31. https://doi.org/10.34068/ijie.14.01.03.

Runcieman, A. (2023). The challenges posed to community/public-service interpreting by the introduction of "plurilingual mediation" in the new companion volume to the Common European Framework of Reference for Languages. *FITISPOS International Journal, 10*(1), 126–137. https://doi.org/10.37536/FITISPos-IJ.2023.10.1.351.

Sato, E., and García, O. (2023). Translanguaging, translation and interpreting studies, and bilingualism. In A. Ferreira and J. W. Schwieter (Eds.), *The Routledge Handbook of Translation, Interpreting and Bilingualism* (pp. 328–45). London: Routledge.

Schwieter, J. W., and Ferreira, A. (2017). *The Handbook of Translation and Cognition*. Malden, MA: Wiley-Blackwell.

Schwieter, J., and Wen, Z. (2022). *The Cambridge Handbook of Working Memory and Language*. Cambridge: Cambridge University Press.

Seeber, K. (2011). Cognitive load in simultaneous interpreting. *Interpreting, 13* (2), 176–204. https://doi.org/10.1075/intp.13.2.02see.

Seleskovitch, D., and Lederer, M. (2002). *Interpréter pour traduire* (4th ed.). Paris: Didier Érudition.

Setton, R. (2012). Models of interpreting. In C. A. Chapelle (Ed.), *The Encyclopedia of Applied Linguistics* (pp. 3722–30). Oxford: Wiley-Blackwell.

Setton, R. (2015). Models. In F. Pöchhacker (Ed.), *Routledge Encyclopedia of Interpreting Studies* (pp. 263–68). London: Routledge.

Shang, X., Russo, M., and Chabasse, C. (2023). Introduction to the special issue Revisiting Aptitude Testing for Interpreting. *The Interpreter and Translator Trainer, 17*(1), 1–6. http://doi.org/10.1080/1750399X.2023.2170042.

Simpson, J. and Cooke, M. (2017) Recognising multilingual realities in ESOL: The NATECLA National Conference 2017 keynote. *Language Issues: The ESOL Journal, 28*(2), 4–11.

Soja, E. (1996). *Thirdspace: Journeys to Los Angeles and Other Real-and-Imagined Places*. Oxford: Basil Blackwell.

Spolsky, B. (1998). *Sociolinguistics*. Oxford: Oxford University Press.

Street, B. V. (1984). *Literacy in Theory and Practice*. New York: Cambridge University Press.

Timarová, Š. (2015), Time lag. In F. Pöchhacker (Ed.), *Routledge Encyclopedia of Interpreting Studies* (pp. 318–420). London: Routledge.

Timarová, Š., Dragsted, B., and Hansen, I. G. (2011). Time lag in translation and interpreting: A methodological exploration. In C. Alvstad, A. Hild, and E. Tiselius (Eds.), *Methods and Strategies of Process Research: Integrative Approaches in Translation Studies* (pp. 121–146). Amsterdam: John Benjamins.

United Nations (2017). *International Migration Report 2017*. New York: United Nations Department of Economic and Social Affairs/Population Division. www.un.org/en/development/desa/population/migration/publica tions/migrationreport/docs/MigrationReport2017.pdf.

Van Lier, L. (2008). Ecological-semiotic perspectives on educational linguistics. In B. Spolsky and F. M. Hult (Eds.), *The Handbook of Educational Linguistics* (pp. 596–605). Malden: Blackwell Publishing.

Verspoor, M., De Bot, K., and Lowie, W. (Eds.) (2011). *A Dynamic Approach to Second Language Development: Methods and Techniques*, vol. 29. Amsterdam: John Benjamins.

Vertovec, S. (2007). Super-diversity and its implications. *Ethnic and Racial Studies*, *30*(6), 1024–54.

Wadensjö, C. (1998). *Interpreting as Interaction*. London: Longman.

Wen, Z. (2016). *Working Memory and Second Language Learning: Towards an Integrated Approach*. Bristol: Multilingual Matters.

Wen, Z. (2021). Language aptitudes. In T. Gregersen and S. Mercer (Eds.), *The Routledge Handbook of Psychology of Language Learning and Teaching* (pp. 389–403). London: Routledge.

Williams, C. (1994). *Arfarniad o ddulliau dysgu ac addysgu yng nghyd-destun addysg uwchradd Ddwyieithog*. [An Evaluation of Teaching and Learning Methods in the Context of Bilingual Secondary Education]. PhD dissertation. University of Wales.

Williams, C. (2002). *Ennill iaith: Astudiaeth o sefyllfa drochi yn 11–16 oed* [A Language Gained: A Study of Language Immersion at 11–16 Years of Age]. Bangor: School of Education.

Xiao, K., and Muñoz, M. (2020). Cognitive translation studies: Models and methods at the cutting edge. *Linguistica Antverpiensia, New Series – Themes in Translation Studies*, *19*, 1–24.

Cambridge Elements ☰

Translation and Interpreting

The series is edited by Kirsten Malmkjær with Sabine Braun as associate editor for Elements focusing on Interpreting.

Kirsten Malmkjær
University of Leicester

Kirsten Malmkjær is Professor Emeritus of Translation Studies at the University of Leicester. She has taught Translation Studies at the universities of Birmingham, Cambridge, Middlesex and Leicester and has written extensively on aspects of both the theory and practice of the discipline. *Translation and Creativity* (London: Routledge) was published in 2020 and *The Cambridge Handbook of Translation*, which she edited, was published in 2022. She is preparing a volume entitled *Introducing Translation* for the Cambridge Introductions to Language and Linguistics series.

Editorial Board

Adriana Serban, *Université Paul Valéry*
Barbara Ahrens, *Technische Hochschule Köln*
Liu Min-Hua, *Hong Kong Baptist University*
Christine Ji, *The University of Sydney*
Jieun Lee, *Ewha Womans University*
Lorraine Leeson, *The University of Dublin*
Sara Laviosa, *Università Delgi Stuidi di Bari Aldo Moro*
Fabio Alves, *FALE-UFMG*
Moira Inghilleri, *University of Massachusetts Amherst*
Akiko Sakamoto, *University of Portsmouth*
Haidee Kotze, *Utrecht University*

About the Series

Elements in Translation and Interpreting present cutting edge studies on the theory, practice and pedagogy of translation and interpreting. The series also features work on machine learning and AI, and human-machine interaction, exploring how they relate to multilingual societies with varying communication and accessibility needs, as well as text-focused research.

Cambridge Elements ☰

Translation and Interpreting

Elements in the Series

Translation and Genre
B. J. Woodstein

Translation as Experimentalism: Exploring Play in Poetics
Tong King Lee

On-Screen Language in Video Games
Mikołaj Deckert and Krzysztof Hejduk

Navigating the Web
Claire Y Shih

The Graeco-Arabic Translation Movement
El-Hussein A. Y. Aly

Creative Classical Translation
Paschalis Nikolaou

Interpreting as Translanguaging
Lili Han, Zhisheng (Edward) Wen and Alan James Runcieman

A full series listing is available at: www.cambridge.org/EITI

Printed in the United States
by Baker & Taylor Publisher Services